Extraordinary Lives

Extraordinary Lives

THE ART AND CRAFT
OF AMERICAN BIOGRAPHY

ROBERT A. CARO / DAVID MCCULLOUGH

PAUL C. NAGEL / RICHARD B. SEWALL

RONALD STEEL / JEAN STROUSE

Edited by WILLIAM ZINSSER

AMERICAN HERITAGE · NEW YORK

Distributed by Houghton Mifflin Company, Boston

This lecture series and book were conceived and produced by Book-of-the-Month Club, Inc. The club would like to thank Vartan Gregorian, president of The New York Public Library, and David Cronin, coordinator of public education programs, for the Library's gracious collaboration as host of the series.

The poem on pages 86–87 is reprinted by permission of the publishers and the Trustees of Amherst College from *The Poems of Emily Dickinson*, edited by Thomas H. Johnson, Cambridge, Mass.: The Belknap Press of Harvard University Press, Copyright 1951, © 1955, 1979, 1983 by the President and Fellows of Harvard College.

American Heritage, Inc.
60 Fifth Avenue
New York, New York 10011

Library of Congress Cataloging-in-Publication Data
Extraordinary lives.
Based on lectures given at the New York Public Library, winter 1985.
Bibliography: p. 235
Contents: The unexpected Harry Truman/David McCullough—In search of Emily Dickinson/Richard B. Sewall—Living with Walter Lippmann/Ronald Steel—[etc.]
1. Biography (as a literary form) 2. United States—Biography. I. Caro, Robert A. II. Zinsser, William Knowlton.
CT21.E97 1986   808′.06692   86–7867
ISBN 0-8281-1219-3

Contents

WILLIAM ZINSSER

Introduction

This book originated as a series of six lectures. The series was conceived by the Book-of-the-Month Club, co-sponsored by The New York Public Library and held in the Trustees Room of the library—a warm, wood-paneled room that seats several hundred people —on successive Monday evenings in the winter of 1985. All six speakers were the authors of widely admired American biographies, and four of them were already well along on their next book, pursuing quarries as different as J. P. Morgan and Harry Truman.

They were asked to be personal and specific: to tell us how they had gone about writing their previous biography or the one they were now embarked on. What first piqued their interest in the subject? Where did they begin their search, and what unexpected paths —and blind alleys—did it lead them down? What were the obstacles and the satisfactions? Whose version of the truth did they decide to trust, and how did they fit the pieces together into a larger truth that would preserve the integrity of both the writer and the written-about?

Thus prompted, the six authors took us on journeys that were full of startling turns. Though their stories were different, the same themes ran through them all. It was quickly obvious, for instance, that the ability to write is only part of the baggage needed for such inquisitive work. A biographer must also have the insouciance of a psychiatrist or a priest—a talent for being unruffled by quirky behavior—and the patience of a detective. For if the trail is often faint, it's because the trailmaker made a compulsive effort to keep it that way.

"Emily was an artist at covering her tracks," Richard B. Sewall says, describing the roadblocks in his twenty-year search for Emily Dickinson. As a sphinx she was rivaled, however, by Walter Lippmann. His biographer, Ronald Steel, recalls asking Lippmann "the world's simplest question": what did his father do for a living? Lippmann looked at Steel for what seemed like a long time and finally said, "I wouldn't want you to make this book a novel." But the champion of concealment was Lyndon Johnson. "He had an obsession with secrecy," says Robert A. Caro, noting that this trait which so strongly marked Johnson's Presidency was rooted in his youth. "I don't think many people would have gone to the trouble, as he did, of having pages of his college yearbook, which detailed unsavory episodes in his college career, cut out with a razor blade from hundreds of copies of the book." One of the most poignant moments recalled in these talks is the one in which Caro takes Johnson's brother Sam, a very sick old man, out to the house in the Hill Country of Texas where he and Lyndon grew up. There, at the family dinner table, Caro, whose dogged questioning of old-timers has finally made him suspicious of the authorized version of Lyndon Johnson's boyhood, takes Sam Johnson back in time and asks him what really happened.

Again and again, dust is thrown in the eyes of the biographer. Ronald Steel, interviewing Walter Lippmann's acquaintances while Lippmann was still alive, found that "there's an unspoken conspiracy among people not to speak badly of one another if the other person is in a position to return the insult." But even when the subject is safely dead, some member of the family has usually been there to sanitize the script. Paul C. Nagel, chronicler of four generations of the family of John and Abigail Adams, met his nemesis in their granddaughter, Elizabeth C. Adams, who lived into the twentieth century and was almost one hundred when she died. "She spent her life tending the fires of family veneration, carefully burning her daddy's papers. One can almost see where and why she destroyed material, so much did she fear the biographer. . . . I come near to weeping when I think of the Adams papers that were deliberately destroyed, and not only by Cousin Lizzie." Poking in the ashes, Nagel found that this distinguished public family had as its private companion a deep streak of alcoholism, humiliation and despair.

Up against so many guardians of the shrine, the biographer soon learns that seeing is not believing. Consider the written evidence about Mary James, the mother of Henry, William and Alice. Alice's biographer, Jean Strouse, says that Alice made a diary entry at the age of forty describing her mother as an "ever springing fountain of responsive love," a woman of "extraordinary selfless devotion, as if she simply embodied the unconscious essence of wife and motherhood." Brother Henry, matching Alice noun for noun, wrote of his mother: "She was patience. She was wisdom. She was exquisite maternity. One can feel forever the inextinguishable vibration of her devotion." No such divinity, however, was apparent to Jean Strouse, looking with a detective's eye at the results. She points out that all five of Mary James's children were crippled by emotional troubles. Nor does any trace of saintly motherhood turn up in Henry James's writing. "The mothers in his novels," Ms. Strouse says, quoting Henry's great biographer, Leon Edel, "are grasping, selfish, demanding, often terrifying creatures."

What is the biographer to make of such huge gaps

between denial and reality? Ms. Strouse takes her answer from J. P. Morgan: "There are two reasons why a man does anything. There's a good reason and there's the real reason." The modern biographer's task is to find the real reasons.

The first requirement for the search is energy—another current that runs through all of these talks. A biographer must be as fit as an Olympic swimmer. The written records alone are of a magnitude beyond imagining by anyone not engaged in such a masochistic craft. Robert Caro mentions that the Lyndon Johnson Library has thirty-two million documents, "and if you keep going through enough of them you'll eventually come across almost everything." Thirty-two million documents! Paul Nagel mentions that the bulk of the Adams family diaries and letters are stored on 608 reels of microfilm. Richard Sewall mentions that the thousand-odd letters in the Harvard edition of Emily Dickinson's *Letters* are only a small fraction of what she wrote. Where, he wonders, are the rest?

Ronald Steel tells us that he inherited the subject of Walter Lippmann from Richard Rovere, who had originally agreed to edit Lippmann's letters for publication. Rovere discovered, "first with delight and then with mounting horror," that Lippmann's letters alone came to at least fifty thousand, and he backed out (who wouldn't?), leaving Steel not only with all the letters—

"some of which dealt with the most complicated affairs of state and others with matters like replacing faucets and taking care of his laundry"—but also with a half-century's worth of Lippmann columns, articles and books. "I came to fear the way in which he would insidiously take over my life," Steel admits.

But written records are only a start. David McCullough says, "You have to know a great deal that you can't get from books—especially from other people's books on the same subject, or even from letters, diaries and newspaper accounts. You have to know the territory." You can't know Harry Truman if you don't know Jackson County, Missouri, McCullough points out, and in describing his many days in and around Independence he gives us a vivid sense of place and of the nineteenth-century Midwestern values that made Truman who he was. What he also gives us is a portrait of the biographer as reporter, walking the beat, looking and listening.

"Just last weekend," McCullough says, "I was talking to a man—and this is what happens when you're lucky —who grew up on an adjoining farm, and he told me that the first time he saw Harry Truman was when Harry came in with a wagon at threshing time and . . ." The totally unexpected detail that follows says a lot about the young Truman—and also about his biographer, modestly attributing this small gem of information to luck. Good biographers, like good reporters,

make their own luck, and there was something ex-
hilarating about hearing this particular example. We
(the audience) were sitting on a Monday evening in The
New York Public Library—where so many writers sit
and write so many books—and McCullough was telling
us about a man he had tracked down over the weekend
in Missouri who knew Truman seventy years ago. This
was biography as a living process. "I talk to people who
talked to people who came up the Missouri River in the
1840s, when Jackson County was the frontier," McCullough says. "It's that close."

Robert Caro is no less a traveler in a time machine.
"Often, during the seven years I was working on this
book," he says, "I would be working in New York one
day—I might have been working in this very library—
and the next day I would fly to Austin and drive west
into the Hill Country. And it sometimes seemed to me
that I was going from one end of the world to the
other." So different was this world from the urban
Northeast of Caro's upbringing that he finally realized
he could understand it only if he became a part of it.
He moved with his wife to a house on the edge of the
Hill Country and lived there for parts of three years,
"driving to lonely ranches and farms to interview the
people who grew up with Lyndon Johnson."

As a city boy Caro had no conception of what it
meant not to have electricity and why Lyndon Johnson
was so revered when he brought it to the Hill Country

as a young congressman. Caro learned the lesson by one of the oldest of methods: show and tell. Several older farm women happened to mention why they were so badly stooped—it was from carrying water when they were young wives. Caro asked them to demonstrate. What was it like to do a full day's wash when every bucket of water had to be hauled up from an outdoor well seventy-five feet deep? His account of what it was like—as reenacted by these old women and by Caro himself—is eloquent proof that documents can never tell the whole story. You have to go to the territory.

Even when no witnesses are still alive, these biographers convey a sense of place as the shaper of character. Richard Sewall reminds us that in his two-volume biography Emily Dickinson doesn't even get born until the second volume. It has taken him that many pages —and ten years of labor—to prepare his readers for her arrival, to enable them to know "where the baby came from, what she was being born into, and some of the stresses and strains that lay in wait. She was in context." The context, of course, was the town of Amherst, "beyond the boundaries of which no Dickinson was ever completely happy," which in turn was set in the context of New England Puritanism, "all austerity and purpose." Sewall makes us see that Emily was as fully a product of reticent Amherst as Harry Truman was of frontier Missouri.

But no atmosphere is as suffocating as the one that Paul Nagel conjures back when he takes us to the White House of 1825, where Louisa Adams, the wife of John Quincy Adams, considered herself nothing more than a prisoner, excluded and patronized by her husband, spending her days writing bitter journals, letters and plays about the status of women in nineteenth-century America. Nagel tells us that it was while writing his earlier biography, *Descent from Glory*, which traced four generations of Adamses, focusing mainly on the men, that he realized that the family had in its women an even more remarkable portrait gallery. To tell their stories would be to get inside the minds of a succession of unusual American women over a hundred-year period, from 1789 to 1889, when "the place of the female in society changed significantly." Considerable courage bobs up in these narratives, along with stirrings of feminism, but what links them is a thread of loneliness, frustration and pain. Nagel, no stranger to irony after immersing himself in the Adams family, starts his journey as their biographer with a single powerful image: the First Lady as captive in the presidential mansion. He gives us a sense of place.

Research, however, is only research. After all the facts have been marshaled, all the documents studied, all the locales visited, all the survivors interviewed, what then? What do the facts add up to? What did the life mean? This was the central question for the six biographers, and to hear them wrestling with it was to begin to see where the craft crosses over into art.

The question is full of traps, some of them ethical. How much right does the biographer have to interpret somebody else's life, to put his own truth on it, to guess at "the real reasons"? Other traps are psychological: can the biographer trust his objectivity after years of round-the-clock living with a saint who turns out to be only human? Judging from these talks, the relationship between the biographer and his subject is the most intimate one in the world of letters, both affectionate and adversarial, as delicately strung with tensions as a long marriage. Jean Strouse recalls that at one point she got so mad at Alice James that she couldn't continue writing. It helped her to remember that Erik Erikson had the same trouble with Gandhi. Ronald Steel, respecting but not always admiring Walter Lippmann, says, "Lippmann knew that in some sense I held his life in my hands."

Such perils have not always accompanied the form. Historically, the purpose of biographies was to bring the good news, to paint a life that was exemplary. Jean Strouse tells us that J. P. Morgan's Christmas present from his mother in 1845, when he was twelve, was a biography of George Washington. We can safely assume that it was favorable. David McCullough tells us that when Harry Truman was nine his mother gave him a four-volume set called *Great Men and Famous Women*, which he loved. His favorite chapter was the one about Robert E. Lee, which included a letter that Lee wrote to his son commending traits of character to the boy that anyone would recognize in the grown-up Harry Truman ("Frankness is the child of honesty and courage").

Lytton Strachey, of course, changed the ground rules of biography in 1918 with his acerbic *Eminent Victorians*, and the Strachean notion that nothing is sacred has been a hallmark of the century ever since; today, no polyp in the famous goes unexamined by the press. Amid such "pitiless scrutiny of public figures," Paul Nagel says, "the biographer is hard-pressed to remain an artist. Both he and the public might well ask: how much disclosure can we witness before we are overcome by trivia, boredom and poor taste? The question is hard to answer if one believes, as I do, that the reader should have the complete story if a biography is to explain adequately how a life and a personality came and went."

Telling the complete story often means dismantling the one that already exists. Richard Sewall, approaching Emily Dickinson with the deference of a novice biographer, found her wrapped in layers of myth and cliché: the Moth of Amherst, the New England Nun, the Queen Recluse. Unwrapped, the woman turned out to be far more interesting than any of the labels—

"a figure of awesome complexity." But to bring that figure to life required a feat of reconstructive surgery. As Sewall once recalled, he had to "fill out the hints she dropped, be discursive where she was elliptical; give her a lineage, a background and foreground; a believable family, home and friends; an education, culture and (above all) a vocation—in the richest possible profusion of detail."

This is the act of intellect that keeps the biographer going: to give coherence to what would otherwise be only data. Ronald Steel says that he constantly found himself dealing with material that didn't make sense to him. Intellectually, it was baffling. Why did Walter Lippmann take various positions that didn't seem to square with what he believed? "I felt that I simply had to pull the material together," Steel says, "and also give some indication of what I thought about it. I don't really believe in facts—I don't think they exist in any significant way. I think that reality is not about facts, but about the relationship of facts to one another."

How six biographers found that relationship is the subject of this book.

These talks were tape-recorded, and so were the lively questions and answers that followed them—exchanges that provided some of the most engaging moments of the series, sending the speakers off on flights of anecdote and memory, often highly personal, that added a new dimension to what they had already told us. In editing this book I worked from the transcripts of the tapes. Almost all oral material needs a certain amount of tidying for publication—the ear makes assumptions and connections that the eye needs to have clarified—and I have done whatever stitchery seemed necessary. Matters of fact and historical record, often mentioned only glancingly in a talk, have also been nailed down: names, dates, titles, events—scholarship, however informally presented, should be useful to scholars who later encounter it in print. But I haven't tried to turn the talks into prose. My aim was to preserve the voice, the rhythms and the vitality of the speakers. What you see, in other words, is very close to what you would have heard if you had been at The New York Public Library on six Monday evenings in the winter of 1985. Listen, therefore, as you read. You will hear about some extraordinary lives.

DAVID McCULLOUGH

The Unexpected Harry Truman

It's hard to imagine a President of the United States with more on his mind than Harry Truman in the first two weeks after the death of Franklin Roosevelt, in April 1945. He found himself suddenly the commander in chief of a two-ocean war, the greatest war in history. He had to bury Franklin Roosevelt—go to Hyde Park with the body and bury him. He had to go up to the Hill and address Congress. He had to meet the press twice in two weeks. He had to meet with his cabinet, which was really Franklin Roosevelt's cabinet, and assure them that he intended to carry on the policies of the New Deal. He had to decide whether to proceed with the United Nations, and he had to address the United Nations upon making that decision, which he did by radio. And, as we all know, he was confronted with the news, for which he had had no preparation, of the existence of the atomic bomb. There were five hundred thousand people involved in the production of the bomb, yet Harry Truman was among those who knew next to nothing about it, until informed by Henry Stimson, the secretary of war.

He also had to see his family relocated in Blair House, before Mrs. Roosevelt moved out of the White House. And he had to adjust to the fact that he, Harry Truman, from Jackson County, Missouri, was President of the United States.

Well, in those same weeks he received a number of letters from Jackson County, Missouri, from his beloved sister, Mary Jane. They were addressed to Blair House, 1651 Pennsylvania Avenue, and they came every two or three days. They were written, as were Mr. Truman's own letters, in a very clear, forthright Jackson County hand. I thought I would begin tonight by reading you a few excerpts:

April 24, 1945

Dear Harry:
We have received so much mail I cannot remember all the details. . . . I am trying to answer some myself. . . . I intend to go into your office and lock the door and keep at it until we get it all done . . . .We try to read all about what you are doing and have kept up pretty well so far. [When she refers to "we" she's referring to Mamma Truman and herself.]

I've lost seven pounds the last week, but no wonder, breakfast is the only meal we have had on time since you went into office. . . . Someone called for pictures yesterday of Mamma, said he was an artist from Washington. I told him I was sorry but Mamma had had all the pictures she could pose for at present.

Now the theme that runs through these letters is what a tremendous disservice Harry has done to them by becoming President of the United States. Here's another:

May 1

Dear Harry:
I do hope you can come [home for Mother's Day on May 11], but if not, I feel sure we can persuade Mamma to make the trip. [In other words, they will come to Washington.] And please tell me if you have any suggestions to make about what you would like me to bring in the way of clothes, for I want to look my best and also get Mamma fixed up all right too and it's a pretty large order on such short notice. . . .

May 7. This is a wonderful letter:

Dear Harry:
I arrived home yesterday and found Mamma well and very much inclined to go to Washington Friday if possible. I had planned to go in today ["in" means into

Kansas City] to get whatever is necessary, but it's pouring down rain and I have lost my voice, so Dr. Graham said I should stay in. Why do such things have to happen when I have so much to do? I'm *hoping* and *hoping* that I can get everything ready to go Friday. However, you call me Wednesday instead of me putting the call through. If you can, call as early as you can, for if I cannot go shopping tomorrow and Wednesday I don't see how I can get it all done.

Here is Harry Truman's answer. He said, "You both have done fine under this terrible blow."

Harry Truman lived seventy years of his life in Jackson County, Missouri. Think of that. He didn't come to Washington until he was fifty years old. Then he was in Washington as a senator and as Vice-President and President for another twenty years. And *then* he went back to Jackson County after he left the White House for another twenty years. So it stands to reason that if you want to understand Harry Truman you'd better know a good deal about Jackson County, Missouri, and you'd better know a good deal about the people there who mattered to him, not just when he was growing up, but during his whole life.

I believe very strongly that the essence of writing is to know your subject. An obvious statement, to be sure. Beginning writers are endlessly encouraged to "write about what you know." But it's the task of a biographer or a historian to know what you write about, to get beneath the surface. You have to know enough to know what to leave out. You have to know enough so that as you're writing, everything is second nature. And you have to know a great deal that you can't get from books—especially from other people's books on the same subject, or even from printed records, such as letters, diaries and contemporary newspaper accounts.

You have to know the territory. You have to go to the place. There is an argument today that all the presidential libraries ought to be unified in Washington under the umbrella of the National Archives. Why should scholars have to go all the way to Independence, Missouri, to work on Harry Truman? I believe it's *essential* to go to Independence, Missouri, to work on Harry Truman. For example, if you sit in the research library at the Truman Library, you look out the window and there are Bess and Harry's graves directly in front of you. And beyond, rising over the trees, is the town water tower, the classic Midwestern water tower, with INDEPENDENCE written on it. And to sit there, as I have, many days, and look out and see people from all over, from other countries, standing and quietly studying the two simple graves, with the label of Independence in the background, particularly if those people are Japanese—it gives one a sense of needing to know what it was that made that man the way he was.

Why did he turn out as he did? Who was Harry Truman? Why didn't he turn out to be George F. Babbitt? Why didn't he turn out to be Warren G. Harding? The American small town, as we know from Sherwood Anderson and Sinclair Lewis and other writers, is not necessarily an ennobling or a purifying experience for a young person growing up.

What was there in his background, in his family, in his education, in the extraordinary life that he lived? If someone were to invent as a work of fiction the life of Harry Truman, no editor would accept it. Too unbelievable that he, of all people, would wind up President of the United States. And at such a juncture in history! I think his Presidency marks the dividing line between our time and another time that was very different. There isn't a day goes by that some headline in the papers doesn't relate back to the Truman administration. Consider that Harry Truman was not just the only President who has used an atomic weapon—he was the President who started the CIA, who started the Joint Chiefs of Staff, who started the National Security Council, who set in motion much of the progress we've seen in civil rights. He recognized the new state of Israel. He launched the Marshall Plan, and with his Point Four Program and Truman Doctrine set in motion as national policy certain obligations which, many contend, saved western civilization—or, some would also argue, led to Vietnam.

And he is also right now an enormously popular fellow. Last fall [1984] we saw two candidates running as if they were Harry Truman: one using his train through Ohio, the other holding up the famous DEWEY DEFEATS TRUMAN headline to show he could do what Harry Truman did—fool the world.

And yet Harry Truman in his own Presidency had the lowest standing with the public of any President we've had since they began taking polls. Twenty-three percent—lower than Richard Nixon on the eve of his resignation. It was common to say, "I'm just mild about Harry." Or "To err is Truman." The leader of the Republicans in the House, Joseph Martin, called him the worst President in history. He barely survived the abuse he received from within his own party. The liberal wing wanted to draft Dwight Eisenhower as the Democratic nominee in 1948.

But then, after a while, things began to change. Harry Truman began to become a character. As a consequence of "Give 'em Hell, Harry," James Whitmore's one-man show. As a consequence of Merle Miller's very entertaining oral history, *Plain Speaking*. And because of some of the old pals and pols who liked to tell stories about "good old Harry." He became a kind of cosmic hick. Picturesque. Abrupt. Feisty. Simple.

One of the people I've interviewed in the course of my research is a man named J. C. Truman. He is Harry

Truman's nephew; he looks quite a lot like Harry and has much of that same warmth and good feeling for people that Truman had. I was spending an evening with Mr. J. C. Truman, who lives in Independence, where he taught high school history, and after we had been talking for a while I said, "Let's suppose I had never met Harry Truman and didn't know anything about him and had never seen a photograph of him. How would you describe him to me?" There was a pause, and he said, "Complicated."

Of course we are all more complicated than we appear. Everybody is hard to know, particularly someone in public life. But Harry Truman was a much more complicated and interesting person than most of us have been led to believe. He was far better educated, far more learned, far more placid, calm, conciliatory, thoughtful. He never raised his voice among those who worked for him. He was never known to dress anyone down in the White House, never known to fly off the handle or become abusive. He did not like confrontations. In his own family he was known as "The Peacemaker." (He came from a very, truly "feisty" family.)

He read perhaps as much as any President in this century, or more, and I would include both Theodore Roosevelt and Woodrow Wilson. Ken McCormick of Doubleday, who was the editor of Truman's memoirs, remembers going up to see him at the Waldorf-Astoria Hotel after Truman had left the White House. He arrived early in the morning and the President wasn't up yet, but Mrs. Truman said, "Go right into his bedroom—he'd love to see you, Ken." So Ken walked in, and there was the President, the former President, sitting in a big chair with two stacks of new books on either side of his chair. He had obviously just gone out and bought all those books. Ken said, "Mr. President, as a publisher, I'm so pleased to see that you are buying all those books. I suppose you read yourself to sleep at night." He said, "No, young man, I read myself awake."

He lived almost ninety years. But at heart he remained a nineteenth-century man. He is from nineteenth-century America. He was never really happy with our twentieth century. He didn't like daylight saving time. He didn't like air conditioning. He didn't like the telephone at all; he would use his pen, or pencil. He would far sooner write a letter than use the telephone, and thank goodness. It's why we have the enormous body of material in the Truman Collection in Independence.

But tonight I want to talk about the process of biography, not just about Harry Truman. I've set him up as a model so that you will understand what the subject is.

First, it seems to me, a biographer must genuinely care about his subject, because as biographer you're living with that person every single day. It's as if you were choosing a spouse or a roommate. And since you have to get up your own steam every day, in partnership with your subject, it's also helpful if your subject is someone with a degree of vitality—plain animal, human vitality. In the two subjects I've worked on most recently, there's been no shortage of that: Theodore Roosevelt and Harry Truman. Two men who are so dissimilar in background and in family origin, but so similar in other ways. In their pleasure in people, for example. Somebody told me, "Harry *liked* all those politicians who would get on at every little stop on the 1948 campaign." Small-town politicians who would come aboard the train to meet the President. Everybody else on the train thought this dreary business. Harry loved it.

He believed in the old notion of nineteenth-century progress. Tomorrow is going to be better than today. We'll make it better. He also confounds some of our standard notions about certain past decades. The period right after World War I, for instance. We read Dos Passos, e. e. cummings, Hemingway, Fitzgerald, coming out of the horror of the first war, feeling emotionally dislocated, their patriotism shattered, their sense of futility worn like a crown of thorns. In Truman's letters from the war—in which, incidentally, unlike Hemingway and some of the others, he fought in combat and saw some of the worst of it—there is none of that. And he writes extensively about the war. What does that tell us about the American character in the early 1920s?

Or consider the mystique of the Roaring Twenties, Jay Gatsby with all his beautiful shirts out in the mansion on Long Island. On Twelfth Street in Kansas City, in his haberdashery, Harry Truman was going broke trying to sell those same shirts. No Stutz Bearcats or raccoon coats in his life. A very different picture. And representative.

Now if you're a biographer, how do you get to that man who lived so long ago? You do it, to begin with, by reading what other people have written. And you try to get through all that as soon as you can. My process is to make a detailed chronology of the whole life, almost a working diary of what he was doing year by year—even day by day if it's an important period such as the First World War. (You see, the war transformed Truman. It changed his life forever. For one thing, he never went back to the farm.)

You need to move quickly into what are known as the primary sources—original letters, diaries and documents that date from the time. And in the case of Truman there is a surplus of marvelous material. My editor at Simon & Schuster once suggested that I take on the very large subject of Franklin D. Roosevelt. He pointed out that there was then no good one-volume biography of FDR, and since I had just spent so much time with Theodore Roosevelt it would seem natural to go on to Franklin.

Well, there are many reasons why I didn't do Franklin, but one is that Franklin Roosevelt never put his heart on paper. He never expressed what he really felt or really thought about anything, on paper. You have to resort to conjecture, again and again, with Franklin Roosevelt. That's simply the kind of person he was. Truman, by contrast, poured himself out, year after year for years, never having the slightest idea that he would ever figure in history. He wrote to his mother over and over—even when he goes to Potsdam in 1945 and he's meeting with Churchill and Stalin, and he's the new President and doesn't know much of anything about foreign policy, and he's never before met with people of such consequence. There he is, going back to his room at night, on the lake at Potsdam, writing letters to Mamma and Mary Jane in Grandview, Missouri.

He was deeply attached to Mamma, and to Mary Jane, and to Bess, and to Margaret. Interestingly, this very manly Missouri fellow who made his career in what were then exclusively male occupations—soldiering and politics—had no close male companions. No real confidants, no intimate male friends. But his devotion to those four women and his need for their approval were consistent, and open, and are expressed repeatedly. He thought his mother was one of the finest human beings who ever lived. If ever there was a mamma's boy, it was Harry Truman. He was a little fellow who wore glasses and played the piano when only little girls had piano lessons, who liked to cook or sit in the chair in the kitchen and braid his sister's hair and sing her lullabies, who played no sports, who, as he told Merle Miller, years later, was "a sissy." If there was a fight, he ran from it.

We have a number of other wonderful mamma's boys in our pantheon of American heroes. Douglas MacArthur. Frank Lloyd Wright. Lyndon Johnson. I can't think of a more outstanding mamma's boy than Franklin Delano Roosevelt. But whether being a mamma's boy is detrimental or advantageous depends, I think, almost entirely on the kind of person mamma was. Martha Ellen Truman was an extraordinary woman.

She was the daughter of Solomon and Harriet Louisa Gregg Young. She lived what was essentially a pioneer life. Harry Truman is the last President we will ever have whose background and roots come right out of the American frontier, or what we associate with the American frontier. And to understand the ideology that was so much a part of his character, the point of view, the sense of right and wrong, the sense of how you conduct yourself, you have to understand western Missouri in the nineteenth century, when western Missouri was America's westernmost frontier. To me this is always a striking thing: in my work I talk to people who talked to people who came up the Missouri River in the 1840s—to Jackson County, Missouri, when Jackson County, Missouri, was the frontier. It's that close.

Now western Missouri is a fascinating place and different from what you might think. It isn't just plain Midwestern; it isn't flat and it isn't hick. It's Southern, as much as it is Midwestern. It's hilly. It's rather dramatic, beautiful, green, exuberant country. Wonderful landscape. Wonderful farming country. It was the real "Eden of America" everybody dreamed of.

It is also right side by side with Kansas City. And of course Kansas City is really something. The Twelfth Street where Harry Truman had his haberdashery is the Twelfth Street of "The 12th Street Rag." Kansas City was wide open. Big time. Never boring. And Harry loved it.

Independence, *his* Independence, was rather sleepy. Old-fashioned. Big Victorian houses. Big lawns, big trees. A green country town, with a courthouse in the center. All the places of Truman's life were set out clearly. The church where he meets the girl he loves all his life—meets her in Sunday school. The courthouse where he becomes a county judge, which isn't a judge but a kind of county commissioner, and quite a big job. There's the railroad station, the old-time red-brick railroad station, where you go off to war. Where you come back from war. Where you go off to Washington and come back. I don't think there's any question that the night Harry Truman came back from Washington after Eisenhower had been inaugurated, and there were ten thousand people at the station to greet him, was the greatest moment in his life.

To know your subject it helps to know his neighbors. Sometimes they want to talk to you and sometimes they don't. And sometimes they tell you things that are true, and sometimes they tell you things that aren't. (It's hard to find somebody over sixty years old in Independence, Missouri, who didn't know Harry "very well.")

But what if what they tell you isn't true? If they believe it, or want *you* to believe it, that's interesting and often revealing. The little things you pick up are often enormously important. Sometimes one remark in an interview can change everything. You find that a certain person had a nickname, and you never think of him again the same way.

For instance, Harry had a pal he went to war with named Spencer Salisbury, and afterward they got into the banking business in Independence. Later there were accusations that Spencer was a little crooked, and in time Spencer went to jail (and Truman had something to do with that, too). Well, when you learn, as I did last weekend, that Spencer Salisbury was known in those years as "Snake-eye Salisbury," and you take another look at his photograph, everything begins to have more life in it. That's all a biographer is really trying to do—to bring people and events and other times back to life.

It's said Harry was a simple man. I don't think he was. And he certainly didn't occupy the White House in simple times. He is one of our crisis Presidents. He was himself, in the eyes of many, his own crisis. I'm sure there are many of you in this room who remember the day when you heard that Franklin Roosevelt was dead and you thought, "My God, Harry Truman is President of the United States!"

Most of the country thought that. But most of the people who *knew* him didn't think that. And one of the things I'm discovering—and here is where you feel the excitement of this work—is the person who existed before he was put in the limelight. And in that person you start to see identifiable marks. It is the same man, even if he's only twenty years old. You root around in libraries, and you find things in libraries—things that nobody else has seen. Not long ago I found, in the Truman Library, reports filed in 1904 by a man named A. D. Flintom, in a Kansas City bank, when Harry, age twenty, was working there. And this is what he said about Harry (the fellow who supposedly could never make a success of anything). Notice how much of the Harry Truman we know is described right here:

He is an exceptionally bright young man, a willing worker. We never had a boy in the vault like him before. [His first job was in the vault.] He watches everything very closely, and by his watchfulness detects many errors, which a careless boy would let slip through. He is a young man of excellent character, and good habits, and always at his post of duty, and his work is always up. He is very accurate in the filing of letters, and the boy is very ambitious [that's interesting] and tries hard to please everybody he comes in contact with. I do not know a better young man in the bank than Trueman.

It's spelled T-r-u-e-m-a-n. Trueman.

And there is, indeed, something allegorical about this story. Harry Trueman, from Independence, Missouri. The Missouri independent, from Independence, Missouri. Truman *was* ambitious. He was buying himself suits and a Panama hat. He was making better money than he'd ever dreamed of making, and he was supporting his family. He and his brother had gone to work because his father had lost everything—their house, all their savings—speculating on grain futures. And this proud family, which had a very nice home in Independence, had to leave town in humiliation and move to a little house in Kansas City, in a very modest neighborhood. The best job his father could get was as a night watchman at a grain elevator. So Harry doesn't go to college; he goes to work in the bank. And he's ambitious, and he's a young man of excellent character, good habits, and "his work is always up."

Then his father decides to go back to the farm, and Harry has to quit the bank and help his father on the farm. He doesn't want to do that, not at all. But he remains a farmer for eleven more years. Hard, hard work. Just last weekend I was talking to a man—and this is what happens when you're lucky—who grew up on an adjoining farm. His name is Steven Slaughter. He was one of eight children on a Missouri farm when there was no electricity, no telephones, no plumbing, no tractors—when farming was just about the same as it was in the eighteenth century. Yet this family sent all eight children to college. Steven went to Columbia University, where he majored in history. He had his career here in New York as a photographer, and now he is retired back in Grandview, where the Truman farm is located.

He told me that the first time he ever saw Harry Truman was when Harry came in with a wagon at threshing time, and he remembers him distinctly because he was wearing a white Panama hat. (It was the hat he bought to work at the bank.) And he said he never saw Harry in Bibb overalls. Everybody wore Bibb overalls, but not Harry. That was one concession to farm life he wasn't willing to make.

Steven Slaughter, who is extremely articulate and perceptive, also told me that his father was there when

John Truman, Harry's father, was dying in 1912. He remembers his father coming back very distraught because John Truman had only wanted to tell him how he hated dying a failure. Steven's father had tried to cheer John up, told him he'd been a good neighbor and a good father and a good farmer, he'd raised a fine family, and he should never consider himself anything like a failure. But John Truman said, yes, he was a failure and was dying a failure. Now, of course, his son was hearing that, too.

Once at the farmhouse when his mother had to have an emergency hernia operation, Harry held the lantern. Now imagine: this is a young fellow, with his own mother going under the knife on the kitchen table. This is someone who is not going to cave in easily in the face of adversity.

Today many of the ideas a man like Truman held to don't seem very smart. And certainly they're not fashionable. But they were solid. And irrefutable. Honor your father and mother. Very interesting. In these letters they don't know how to punctuate; they capitalize or they don't capitalize—there seems no rationale to it. But they always capitalize *Mother* and *Father*. Always. Make good on your debts. When Harry Truman went broke with the haberdashery, there was no shame in it locally because lots of people were going broke in the retail trade in Kansas City in the early 1920s—there was an advance tremor of the oncoming depression in the

Midwest. And Harry made good on all his debts. He was still paying them off during his second term in the Senate—it took him that long. You don't buy anything until you have the money to buy it. You work hard because hard work is part of life. If you're working on a family farm you're not working for yourself, you're working for the family. You're working for the good of the whole. Your word is your bond. Your loyalty to your family is absolute, as is loyalty to your friends. And you must be a good neighbor; by definition a good neighbor is somebody you can count on when you're in trouble. He isn't somebody you have cocktails with. But if you're in trouble and you go to him, he drops everything and he helps you.

Lemar, Missouri, south of Independence, is a little, dusty town that doesn't look much different today from what it did in 1884, when Truman was born there. The house where he was born still stands. A tree his father planted to commemorate the great occasion is still growing in the front yard. The room in which he was born is just large enough to hold a bed. A tiny little house, no plumbing, no cellar.

A sister of John Truman's was there visiting, not quite a year later, and a letter she wrote contains the first-known reference to the future President—I think it's wonderful: "Baby is real sick now. He is so cross, we can't do anything."

He did have a temper. He was very stubborn. Which

is traditional, almost obligatory, among the Scotch-Irish, which most all of his people were—those who came out to Missouri from Kentucky—brave, hard-working, devout, mostly Baptist, often narrow, sometimes very prejudiced, sometimes inclined to sudden violence, true pioneers. It was Daniel Boone's son, Daniel Morgan Boone, who led the migration to western Missouri. And during the Civil War western Missouri on the Kansas border became a bloodbath. We have no conception of what went on there; *I* certainly had no idea. I discovered that in the period from John Brown's raid in 1859 until the end of the Civil War, no fewer than twenty-seven thousand civilians were killed in the border war. *Twenty-seven thousand!* That makes it one of the worst civilian disasters ever to happen in this country. Anybody could be taken out of his house, dragged into the woods and shot. Killed. Often literally butchered. Hung up and mutilated. It was vicious guerrilla warfare and Truman's people were right in the middle of it. His mother's family's farm was burned twice. The family was removed from their home by the famous Union Army Order No. 11, which required that all who were not in sympathy with the Union had to leave their land and move to special camps. All of Jackson County was burnt-over territory, and today they still talk about it.

You pick things up spending time on the native ground, taking your time, listening, poking through the old local papers. I found an editorial in an issue of the Independence paper, published in 1901, the year Harry graduated from high school. It made plain that if those uppity Negroes around the square were to continue behaving as they had in the past few days, no one should be surprised if there was a lynching. *That's* Independence, Missouri, too. And when you realize that Truman's people were slaveholders, and that he grew up in a town where the newspaper offered such advice to good citizens, you realize how much more there has to be to the story of his stand on civil rights in 1948. He was the first President since Lincoln, the first President in our century, to make civil rights and racial equality a policy.

Harry Truman is one of those people who figure in history with a capital *H*. But what is much more important is that he was a human being. And we have to know, what kind of human being? Also, what kind of people did he surround himself with? What should we make of the people around Truman, a vitally important question—and not just the Harry Vaughans, the cartoon characters who became the butt of so much ridicule, but the very able people, too. Consider whom he had in his Cabinet, in his administration: Robert Lovett, Dean Acheson, Averell Harriman, George Marshall. Hardly small-time political hacks. What does this say about the biographer's subject? Or the presence on the White House staff of a young man like Clark Clifford—how does he reflect on "the boss"?

Certainly one of the most important events of the Truman administration was the creation of Israel. Clifford is for it, Marshall against it. Then Eddie Jacobson, Truman's old partner in the haberdashery, arrives in Washington. You must understand all these people in order to understand your subject if he's Harry Truman. And it's hard. And it's fascinating. *And it takes time.* You have to know what you're talking about.

It's much more important to listen when you're interviewing people than to worry about what questions you're going to ask. Beginners in this kind of work often make the mistake of going in with a list of questions. Pretty soon the person being interviewed feels that he's filling out a questionnaire. And something happens—it isn't a conversation. A lot of my time is spent in preparing for the interview—to know the subject so well that I know what to listen for and what to ask when the time is right to ask it.

People sometimes say to me, "How can you spend four years writing a book about the Brooklyn Bridge? One subject. Or six years writing a book about the Panama Canal. One subject." I suppose it will take six years or more to write a book about Harry Truman. One subject. It isn't one subject. It's a thousand subjects. And the magic, the sense of adventure, comes from not knowing where you're headed or how you're going to wind up feeling, what you're going to decide. A large part of the task is getting to understand a period and a time. Truman's era starts in 1884, when Chester A. Arthur was in the White House—we had a wooden Navy; it ends in the 1970s. What a time. It's our time, the time we've known.

I saw Truman just once. He was getting out of a car with Averell Harriman in front of the St. George Hotel in Brooklyn. I was on my way home from work. Until then I had only seen pictures of him in the newspapers or had seen him on black and white television. My first thought was, "My God, he's in color!" He seemed to radiate health. (And everybody who knew him has told me that this was very much part of him.) His eyes were greatly magnified by his glasses—I remember that—and very blue. He seemed to be having a good time. I remember that, too.

He had a wonderful time being Harry Truman, the whole way along. He's the only President I know of who was in better health when he came out of the White House than when he went in. And I'm having a wonderful time getting to know him.

The great painter of the nineteenth century, Thomas Eakins, advised his students to try to look deeper into the heart of America. I'm trying to look deeper into the heart of America by looking into the life and times of this one man. And the more I look, the more I keep coming back to J. C. Truman's observation: "Complicated."

———

Q. Erica Jong in yesterday's New York Times Book Review *said that there is autobiography within fiction, and that there is fiction within autobiography. Is there any truth in that?*

A. I agree completely. I think one of the most interesting things about autobiography is what the autobiographer leaves out. I had this brought to my attention in dramatic form in writing my book about Theodore Roosevelt—in fact, it was one of the reasons I wanted to write about him. It suddenly occurred to me that in his autobiography he never mentioned his first wife. You would never know that she existed. Then, further on, I read his account of what happened at Panama, and I realized that he wasn't just leaving his wife out; he was leaving out a lot of other things that were enormously important. If they're leaving it out, it's probably very important.

We look at a chair and we see the solid: we see the chair's shape in the wood. In looking at an autobiography it's as if you're looking at the voids in the chair in order to see the form. Look at what the author is not telling you. I suppose the fact that a person will even write an autobiography is revealing. I doubt that

Abraham Lincoln would have ever written an autobiography. There is always some self-serving going on. I like the autobiographical writings of people that are written before they become celebrated. Because afterward you can't help but be a little suspicious. Because they know that authors— biographers and historians— will someday be reading their letters, that little note they're supposedly writing in the privacy of the home, you know, alone with their conscience. And then they establish a museum in which to put that letter.

Q. *Why did Theodore Roosevelt leave out any mention of his first wife?*

A. It was too painful. He really was head over heels, madly, irrationally in love with her. And her death brought him to such a pass, such a terrible confrontation with a lot of things, including the death of his mother on the same night. He hardly mentions his mother. He can't *not* mention her—I mean, he had to have had a mother. So she gets two or three sentences.

Q. *You mentioned that there was a great dissimilarity between Teddy Roosevelt and Harry Truman, and yet you said they had much in common. Could you go into that?*

A. Both were men of enormous physical vitality. They loved to be physically fit. The famous Truman walks were only part of the regimen he went through; he did exercises, he was a swimmer in the White House pool. He believed in the old adage about a sound mind and a sound body. But he was not an outdoorsman; he took no pleasure in killing anything, and of course Theodore could hardly contain himself, given the chance.

They also were avid readers. As children they were both handicapped by bad eyesight, and as a result they led quite withdrawn, sheltered childhoods. They were both passionately interested in history. I think maybe that's something you're born with. Truman didn't just read American history; he read Greek history, Roman history, European history, all his life. And he remembered it. As did Theodore. Politically they were both mavericks of a kind, though Truman was much more of a ballplayer—going along with the party boys—than TR. Each felt he could tell what the ordinary person thought and felt because he understood the ordinary person; he didn't need to take polls. Actually I think Truman really did understand, because he was one himself.

They were dissimilar, certainly, in background. Truman looked upon both Roosevelts as—to use his word—"fakers." Franklin Roosevelt was the kind of farmer, in Harry Truman's eyes, who had never pulled a weed in his life.

Both men, as grown men, had great physical courage, for all their sissy boyhoods. They had a marked ability to express themselves in plain terms. They weren't orators. Neither one was a very good platform speaker. But both of them knew how to let the audience know what they thought. Perhaps the greatest difference is that TR was a showman. He really loved the theater of politics. Harry Truman was never that; he never had a shred of glamour or, to use that overrated word, "charisma." TR was much more egotistical and flamboyant.

But Theodore is more like Harry Truman than Franklin was. Nothing about Franklin Roosevelt is similar to Harry. Certainly one of the most important things you must do if you're writing a biography of Harry Truman is to understand Franklin Roosevelt, to see the act that Truman follows. William Luchtenberg's marvelous book, *In the Shadow of FDR*, makes the case that virtually all our Presidents have remained in the shadow of FDR, but nobody was in the shadow more than Harry Truman, and to come out of the shadow was a great necessity for him. He never expressed his dissatisfaction with Roosevelt publicly—you have to read between the lines to see that it's there—and he wouldn't have expressed it, because Roosevelt was his commander in chief, Roosevelt was the leader of the party, Roosevelt was the President. Roosevelt was also a successful politician, and Harry Truman wanted always to be a successful politician. It was the only line he knew. That was his job.

A preacher who lives next door to the Truman house in Independence told me how he and Harry would go on walks, after Truman came home from Washington. There's an enormous gingko tree on the street, just around the corner from the Truman house—it must be the biggest tree in Independence—and the preacher said that every time Truman walked by this tree he would talk to it. I asked him, "What did he say?" He said Truman would say, "You're doing a good job."

Q. Would you talk about Truman's involvement with the Pendergast machine?

A. That's a big point, of course. Truman got into politics, and was successful in politics in Jackson County for the first twenty-odd years of his political career, because he was in association with Boss Pendergast of Kansas City, a very tough, *very successful* political boss. One of the great bosses of the boss era.

The explanation in Jackson County—and I think it makes sense—is that Pendergast needed Truman as much as Truman needed Pendergast. Captain Harry Truman came home from the war a very popular man. He had led Battery D through some of the toughest fighting in France and with little loss of life. Most of his men were from Kansas City, most were Irish Catholics, and Truman of course was neither Irish nor Catholic. But they adored him. And Tom Pendergast heard about this fellow, Harry Truman, who also had a great, big interconnected family out in the surrounding country. If the family would vote for him, and Battery D would vote for him, he was probably well on his way.

So he picked Truman—and this is greatly oversimplifying the point—as window dressing for an essentially corrupt regime. Truman said that Pendergast never asked him to do anything unethical or illegal. I'm not sure yet whether he did or didn't. When Pendergast went to prison, federal investigators went through all the evidence—the books, everything in the Jackson County courthouse that Truman ran—and found that not a dime had been taken, nothing had been done illegally. When the 1948 presidential campaign came along, the Republican party did the same thing, concerning Truman's Senate career.

No senator that I've talked to, nobody I've talked to who was in government in Washington when Truman was senator, has ever suggested that there was anything crooked about Harry Truman. Quite the reverse. If you read Allen Drury's wonderful nonfiction book about the Senate, which was written in the forties, the observations about Harry Truman, who was still just a senator, are entirely complimentary, very revealing. As some of you remember, Truman made his name as a senator with the Truman Committee, the committee charged with rooting out inefficiency, corruption, and graft in the Defense Department. How wonderful if we could reinstate that committee today! The great thing about the Truman Committee was that it had teeth. It could send people to prison, and did. And it saved billions of dollars. It saved a sum that was equivalent to about half the cost of the Marshall Plan. Imagine that! After the war, journalists in Washington made up a list of the ten men in civilian life who had done the most for the war effort, and Harry Truman was the only member of either house in the legislature who was on the list. He was a highly effective senator in that term because Pendergast was gone by then. In the previous term, when Pendergast was still in power, he didn't really do very much. He was still in the shadow of the boss.

Q. Will you tell us something about your research methods—organizing your material and interviewing people?

A. I have a filing system where I file all the subjects the book is going to cover—the Truman Committee; Independence, Missouri; World War I; and so forth—drawers of subject files, and everything I find on any of the given subjects goes into that file. Then there's a biographical file, on every character of any consequence who will appear in the book—hundreds of people eventually. It's as if you're building a detective case. In some ways you're like a lawyer going out taking depositions—you're hunting down witnesses and getting their view.

Almost everybody wants to be interviewed, and in fact they often don't want you to leave. Often you go back several times. Sometimes they don't want to be taped. You can quickly tell whether they're self-conscious about that. Lawyers, I find, don't like to be taped. If you're not taping them they can always say,

"You misquoted me." One prominent member of Truman's official family, a lawyer, told me virtually nothing during my first interview. The next time I didn't take the tape recorder, and he told me quite a lot. Many people are protective. They're not only protecting their own reputation; they're protecting the reputation of your subject. They don't want to tell you anything that will look detrimental and that they will be held responsible for.

It's easy to get people talking about what they experienced, what they saw, what they knew. But you've got to know when to hear a name that means something, and make the connection, and you've got to stop them every now and then, particularly if they've been interviewed on the subject many times, because they've often developed a spiel—you know, "I'll give you my Harry Truman #A6, designed for biographies."

One thing that makes my subject so interesting is that, for all that's been written and published about Harry Truman, almost all of it is autobiographical in spirit. Harry Truman's own memoirs, of course, are autobiographical. *Plain Speaking*, Merle Miller's book, is the elderly Harry Truman talking about Harry Truman. The very good book that his daughter, Margaret, wrote, a delightful book, is nonetheless written by an adoring and loyal and partisan member of the family. The last biography of Truman of any real consequence, my favorite biography, is Jonathan Daniels'

The Man of Independence, which was published in 1950 while Truman was still President. So the opportunity to write a biography of Truman is unlimited.

Also, I think you have to aim high. You have to say to yourself, I'm going to try to write the definitive biography of Harry Truman, and you always have to tell yourself that what you write is going to be in print for a very long time. So be careful. Be honest. Take the reader into your confidence. If you don't really know something, if you're hypothesizing, be honest about it. Say so.

Q. I'm interested to know how you could leave Teddy Roosevelt where you left him, and to what degree you're going to take him up again? [McCullough's "Mornings on Horseback" ends before TR becomes President.]

A. I take that as a compliment. I probably won't take him up again, because my intention in that book was to try to do something that was an exercise in form. I wanted to see if I could capture the person without going into the personage of history. So I wanted to end when TR was formed as a person—when he's about to step onto the stage of history as a character in history and henceforth so very often self-conscious. And I was also trying to do something that I'm trying to do with the Truman book. Let me explain it very quickly.

Biography is the story of the evolution of an individual, and often you see that person change and grow—grow spiritually, grow physically, grow in his or her career, grow as a consequence of some terrific conflict or ordeal. Now in most biographies, one of the main reasons you see them grow and change is because the supporting cast *doesn't* change. The brother, the sister, the father, the mother, the partner in business, whatever, are given to you as fixed types. They are like identifiable marks on the landscape, against which you see the transition of the main character's passage. But life isn't like that. The supporting cast, the minor characters, are also changing, sometimes more than the main character, and how they're changing is affecting the growth of the main character. So you have to understand them all. I have to understand Mary Jane Truman, Harry's sister, you see.

Incidentally, I haven't even touched on the importance of photographs. The use of photographs in this work is vital, essential. Too many academically trained historians and biographers don't use photographs enough. I just found at the Truman Library a marvelous collection of photographs taken at the Truman farm just before World War I, when a whole way of life in America was about to vanish forever. And in those photographs you see, among other things, that Mary Jane Truman was a lovely-looking woman, a really beautiful woman. But she has always been portrayed as a pathetic old maid who never married, who stayed home and took care of Mamma: plain Mary Jane. I've had to change my views about Mary Jane. It's easy to see in her face why so many people admired her and liked her, and of course you wonder, why did she never marry? Was she really staying there taking care of Mamma, in order for Harry to be off doing what he did? Did Harry, in a sense, walk out on them by going to war, when he was past thirty, when his eyes were bad, when farmers were being urged by President Wilson to stay on the farm? Did he walk out on them when he married Bess Wallace, who had an elegant way of life, who lived in one of the largest houses in Independence, and whose mother let it be known that Harry wasn't good enough for her daughter? (I once asked Harry Truman's sister-in-law, Mrs. May Wallace, if it was true that Mrs. Wallace didn't think Harry was good enough for Bess. She said, "Oh, yes, that's absolutely true. But you have to understand that Mrs. Wallace didn't think *anybody* was good enough for Bess.")

Q. Could you touch on your psychological identification with the subject?

A. Nobody's ever asked me that before. I'll tell you two things. One is that my father looks very much like Harry Truman. The second is that I can remember waking up early in the morning to get ready to go to high school, and my father was shaving, and I hadn't stayed up to hear the final returns of the election, and I said to him, "Who won?" and he moaned, "Truman." He was very down about that.

More important, I'm from Pittsburgh, which is more

Midwestern than Eastern. I'm very interested in the frontier and its effect on the whole American experience, the American character. Another thing, I'm drawn to Truman because he's authentic. Today—and I'm not just talking about Reagan, but about anyone who is going to be President from now on—we're seeing a Presidency that's done mainly with mirrors. Truman was the last President who knew everything that was going on that had to do with the executive office. He presented his own budget and had a press conference in which he was grilled on the budget. No President could do that today. He was largely what he appeared, and I think that's one of the reasons people are so charmed by him now.

This evening we're in a library—a library that I'm more indebted to than I can possibly express. I did the research for my first two books here. And in closing I just want to say that I don't think you could find any President, or young man, who was more influenced by books than Harry Truman, all of his long life. When he was nine years old his mother—and they weren't affluent people, to say the least—spent a lot of money for four volumes of books called *Great Men and Famous Women,* published in 1894. The fact that Truman had these books as a little boy, and read them, has been commented on by other writers many times. But I don't know if anybody ever bothered to read those books to see what's in them. I did. And they're wonderful. They are mostly chapters from magazines of the time, like *Harper's,* and from European publications. They're terrific—lucky the child who could have such books today.

Because the Trumans were Southern in their attitudes they revered Robert E. Lee. At one point Harry gave his mother a little portrait of Robert E. Lee and she hung it beside her dresser. Harry's favorite biographical essay in these books was on Robert E. Lee, and it included a letter that Lee wrote to his son in 1860. Imagine the little boy, Harry, out there in Jackson County reading this, and notice how much of it is what he tried so hard to live up to.

Lee writes: "You must be frank with the world. Frankness is the child of honesty and courage." (Very interesting idea.) "Just say what you mean to do on every occasion, and take it for granted you mean to do right. If a friend asks you a favor, you should grant it, if it is reasonable. If not, tell him plainly why you cannot. You will wrong him and wrong yourself by equivocation of any kind. Never do a wrong thing to make a friend or keep one." And this is the great line: "Above all, do not appear to others what you are not."

He never did that. Like him or not, he never did that. And I'm trying to find out, who was Harry Truman?

RICHARD B. SEWALL

In Search of
Emily Dickinson

Emily Dickinson could cut your head off with a re-mark. When I was in the early stages of writing her biography I ran across a few that put me on my guard. There was the one about the old lady who came to the door to ask about rentals in Amherst. Emily said, "I directed her to the cemetery to save her the trouble of moving." Another, which came closer to home, was a remark she made after reading a biography of George Eliot: "Biography first convinces us of the fleeing of the biographied." That had a frosty sound, but my search was under way, and I couldn't turn back.

In the beginning I didn't go searching for Emily Dickinson; she went searching for me. When I first taught Emily Dickinson's poetry at Yale in the 1930s, I had no idea she would one day run my life. At that time I had no trouble running hers. I blush when I think of the clichés I fell for: the Frustrated Lover, the Great Renunciation, the Queen Recluse, the New England Nun, the Moth of Amherst; a father straight out of *The Barretts of Wimpole Street*; the tense little lyrics whose chief end and aim was to send chills up and down the spine. It was like teaching Robert Burns as the simple farmer whistling behind his plow.

It was the Age of Innocence, untroubled by Freudians, Feminists, New Critics, Structuralists, or Deconstructionists. We sailed along serenely with no reliable critical text, not even a decent Collected Poems or Collected Letters. George Whicher's *This Was a Poet* (1938), following the centennial tributes (1930) of Genevieve Taggard and Josephine Pollitt, seemed to do it up fine for biography. In the 1930s it was T. S. Eliot who had us all agog. While we were puzzling ourselves silly over "The Love Song of J. Alfred Prufrock," the serious critical work on Emily Dickinson you could put in your eye. She was no particular problem. There were plenty of poems that made enough sense for rich teaching, and the puzzling ones I let slip by. It was a garden path for a young sentimentalist.

Then, in 1945, came an important volume, *Bolts of Melody*—660 hitherto unpublished poems by Emily Dickinson, edited by Millicent Todd Bingham, the only child of Mabel Loomis Todd, who was the original editor of Dickinson's poems and letters in the 1890s. Shortly after its publication a senior colleague of mine at Yale, Professor Stanley Williams, dropped by my office and asked, rather casually, if I'd like to review it. He would have done it himself, he said, but he was too busy—a remark that tells a lot about how Emily Dickinson stood at that time in the eyes of professional academics. Too busy indeed! So he farmed it out to one of the youngsters. If 660 new Dickinson poems hit the streets tomorrow, there'd be a scramble you wouldn't believe.

I had never reviewed a book in my life, but I swallowed hard and said I'd do it. It turned out to be a milestone in my career. I was puzzled by many of the poems (I still am), so I wrote mostly about the quality of the editing, which, when I compared it with what I had been using, struck me as the best so far. That was faint praise, but it pleased Mrs. Bingham. She asked me, in a pleasant note, to join her for lunch at the Cosmopolitan Club in New York City. And the search—though I didn't know it—was on.

What I didn't know was that Mrs. Bingham had been searching for someone to write a biography of Emily Dickinson. It took a good five years for the full truth of her intentions to come out. During that time we corresponded intermittently, we had family picnics in Maine, and once I went to see her in Washington, D.C. At each meeting, as I see it now, another carrot was dangled in front of this uncomprehending donkey —a manuscript, a curio, an anecdote. Then, one summer day on Hog Island, Maine, about 1951, she put the question: "Why don't you do something on Emily Dickinson?" I asked what. "A biography," she said, with a perfectly straight face. "Why?" I asked. "Aren't there enough in the field already?" Then came a startling answer: "Richard, they don't know a thing." It took me another five years to see what she meant. Yes, they knew a thing, even two. But what they knew had to be reassessed in the light of what she knew and—this is the point—could document. Gradually the whole story came out: her mother's affair—that's a very pale word for it—with Emily's brother Austin, the full extent of which even she didn't know until she was over fifty. (It is now admirably described in Polly Longsworth's book *Austin and Mabel: The Amherst Affair.*) Mrs. Bingham had documentary material that staggered the imagination: her mother's letters to and from Austin, hundreds of them; her mother's diaries and journals; Austin's diary, and various miscellaneous items that she was fond of calling "primary source material of first importance."

Her mother's story had been a great burden to her. It may not have ruined her life, but it surely saddened the last thirty years. The gossip had run on too long, and she wanted, as she put it, "to set the record straight." Apparently all those in the know—that excluded me—had known for a long time what she had in her archive. She once recalled Bernard DeVoto's remark as they emerged together from a New York theater: "Millicent" (and no one less than a Bernard DeVoto could call her that), "when are you going to come clean?"

She wanted the whole story told, but told in the larger context of Emily Dickinson's life. At every turn this was her insistence. The story was important as it threw light, however indirectly, on a great poet's life and work.

Even after I knew the whole truth I was full of disclaimers and misgivings. I had never done anything like this before. I was unprepared in Dickinsoniana. And about that time I had committed myself to writing a book on tragedy. This excuse didn't work any better than the others. "Tragedy!" exclaimed Mrs. Bingham. "What a preparation! Tragedy on Main Street!" What could I do? At that time Jay Leyda, who had been working with Mrs. Bingham on her archive and was just rounding out his monumental two-volume study, *The Years and Hours of Emily Dickinson*, came all the way from New York to New Haven to say, "You'd better do it." I protested again. I said, "Why not you, Jay? You know more about Emily Dickinson than any-one else in the world." He said he wasn't interested. "I collect the facts," he said. "It's up to you people to make something of them." I was hooked.

Then came the long, slow process of catching up with the field. Mrs. Bingham and Jay were generous

with advice, coinciding nicely on one point—a point
that still needs heavy underscoring. They reminded me
that there was only so much primary source material.
There were the poems and the letters, now well edited
by Thomas Johnson and Theodora Ward (1955 and
1958). There were the family documents in Mrs. Bingham's *Emily Dickinson's Home* (1955). There was Jay
Leyda's *Years and Hours.* And there was what remained in Mrs. Bingham's archive that she hadn't used
in *Emily Dickinson's Home* and that she had pledged Jay
not to use in his *Years and Hours.* "All else," she declared with great emphasis, "is conjecture."

As to her mother's story, she urged objectivity. "You
have heard only one side of it—my side," she said.
"Now get the other one." "Supposing," I said, "after
I've gone through all the material I conclude that your
mother was an unscrupulous flirt who wrecked another
woman's marriage?" Quick as a flash she said, "Then
you'll have to say so."

She insisted on scrupulous accuracy. As the first
woman Ph.D. in geography from Harvard, she was
trained in accuracy—as I heard her say a dozen times
—"to the fifth decimal place." During the First World
War she lectured to the French general staff (in France
and in French) on problems of terrain in certain combat areas. She knew their country better than they did.
She was a stickler. Once, when I was well on with the
biography, I read to her a draft of the chapters about

her mother and Austin. (I was on thin ice!) We were sitting in her cottage in Maine; it was after lunch and we had worked hard all morning. She was then about eighty. I thought I caught her nodding off to sleep. Not at all. Suddenly her head came up. She said, "Richard, the lady whom you have just referred to as Mrs. Edward Tuckerman happens to have been Mrs. Frederick Tuckerman. They were two very different people. Do not confuse them." Next day, same situation. Again the head came up. "In the last four pages you have used *exemplary* twice. I think once is enough." So be it.

But once I caught her. In *Emily Dickinson's Home* she has Edward Dickinson, Emily's father, as valedictorian of his class at Yale, 1823. Just to be sure, I went to the Yale memorabilia room in Sterling Library, got out the commencement program for the class of 1823, and discovered, not without a little grim satisfaction, that Edward Dickinson never made it. He was an also-ran. The valedictorian was some unknown from New Jersey. Be that as it may, she was a remarkable woman. In telling her mother's story she was biased and knew it. But in the bread-and-butter matter of scholarship—names, dates, historical details—she was all but infallible. She saved me from many a slip.

All this—the Mrs. Tuckermans, Edward as valedictorian—happened rather late in the game. I want to say some more about the catching-up process. Without two sabbaticals I would have been nowhere. Without a forbearing wife I would have been lost. For our first sabbatical, in 1959–1960, we rented a chalet above Innsbruck, Austria, to the consternation of one faculty wife whose husband spent his sabbaticals and most of his summers in the British Museum. "Why Innsbruck for Emily Dickinson?" she asked in dismay. "Why, don't you know?" replied my wife. "Emily laid out the original ski trails. Richard is very thorough. He must try them out."

I spent the winter on nothing but the letters and the poems, plus a turn or two on the slopes now and then. Gradually the clichés of the 1930s came to seem more and more ridiculous. Our Emily, the Queen Recluse, began to emerge as Dickinson, a figure of awesome complexity. I took notes furiously and kept endless five-by-seven cards, indispensable for someone whose memory is as poor as mine. All this was necessary, as I saw it, for the next step: mastering all the previous biographical studies and the growing body of critical work that had followed the publication in the fifties of the Harvard editions of the poems and letters. There wasn't much of either in the library of the University of Innsbruck. ("Emily *who?*") But I knew they could wait till I got home.

This takes us to the fall of 1960, the year of the publication of Jay Leyda's *Years and Hours* and the year after my book on tragedy was finally published. I wish

I could say that my sabbatical year had put me in command of the Dickinson situation, or even brought me to the point where I knew where I was going. But it didn't do either.

I should add that Emily Dickinson herself was almost no help. She was very secretive (was it a family trait or simple New England reticence?) about almost everything a biographer wants to know. She was an artist at covering her tracks. She never dated a poem and she gave titles to only a handful of them. She followed the advice of one of her poems: "Tell all the truth. But tell it slant. Success in circuit lies." She was a master at circuitry, and I think she enjoyed it. "In a life that stopped guessing," she wrote her sister-in-law, "you and I would not feel at home." One of her poems begins: "The Riddle we can guess/ We speedily despise."

Well, she left us plenty to guess at—and riddle after riddle to puzzle over. Her favorite device was metaphor —that is, telling something in terms of something else. She even played that game with her best friends in some of her most intimate letters. When she was nineteen she wrote a letter to her beloved confidante, Jane Humphrey, an Amherst girl, in which a mysterious "gold thread . . . a long, big shining fibre" wove in and out of a passage that, deciphered, may be announcing nothing less than the beginnings of the poet in her, the call to be a poet. But would she tell Jane straight out? No, she challenged Jane to figure it out. "What do you weave from all these threads?" she wrote. "Do you dream from all this what I mean?" Why couldn't she simply, in Bernard DeVoto's words, "come clean"? It would have made it so much easier for all of us. But a lot less interesting.

So, after that first sabbatical, I saw how elusive my quarry was, how far off the old generalities were. Back in New Haven, I was faced with the immediate problem of beginning; the period of gestation couldn't go on forever. Something had to get off those five-by-seven cards and on to paper. How to begin? I had always shuddered at biographies that began, "It was a clear, cold morning in mid-December 1830, when the cry of a newborn baby broke the winter stillness." And once you begin, how to tell the story of a life that had no story? I was reminded of Clifton Fadiman's remark about Henry James: "Nothing happened to him except everything." That is, it happened inside, which makes it hard for biographers. And James's life was eventful compared with Emily Dickinson's. He shuttled from continent to continent; he was wined and dined; he had a public life; you can distinguish clearly between his early novels and his late ones. But with Dickinson there is no narrative structure on which to pin an account of her life. Her letters, beginning at age eleven, do show marked development over the years. But it has often been remarked that the early poems are very much like the late poems. And any attempt to divide the canon into, say, early, middle and late periods must face the fact that precise dating of any of the poems is almost impossible. (In the collected edition there is a "c," for *circa*, after the date on every poem.) In short, the old formulas for writing literary biography were inapplicable. I was stuck.

I made many false starts. Most notable was the "literary origins," or genetic, approach—very academic and scholarly. When was she born poetically, intellectually, spiritually? Where did she get her pitch? From the romantics? She herself spoke of Keats and the Brownings. But didn't she go back farther? To Donne and Herbert, the seventeenth century? Clearly her greatest literary enthusiasms were Shakespeare and the Bible. But she never expanded on either—mostly quotation and aphorisms. Of Shakespeare she said, "Why is any other book needed?" Of the Bible, "It stills, incites, infatuates—blesses and blames in one. Like Human Affection, we dare not touch it, yet flee, what else remains?" Among important origins, one must include Isaac Watts, the great writer of hymns, whose meters provided Dickinson with her characteristic form. Then there are Emerson, Thoreau, Hawthorne, all living parts of the culture she grew up in. A bold first attempt had me starting with a synthesis of all these, until a discerning and witty friend intervened with a thunderous "This will never do." He was right. The genetic approach was not for me. The synthesis went into the fire. How good it is to have discerning friends! Let me give you another example. I had just finished a first draft of the chapter on the Master Letters—those three incomparable love letters, each with the salutation "Master," a figure whose identity is still one of those puzzles. Jay Leyda happened to be in New Haven that winter as a visiting professor of film just after I had written that chapter, and I gave it to him for comment. I waited for a week. Finally we arranged a lunch. We had soup. No comment. We had salad. No comment. We had dessert. No comment. I couldn't stand it any longer. "Jay," I said, "what did you think of that chapter?" His answer was six words: "Do you enjoy being a sleuth?"

I got the message. I had been concerned with ferreting out the mysterious master: the Reverend Charles Wadsworth? Samuel Bowles? Thomas Wentworth Higginson? Judge Otis Phillips Lord of Salem, with whom later on we know she was in love? I had been preoccupied with detective work and not with the documents themselves—the human documents, those extraordinary, passionate, pleading, witty, nervy, tactless, beautiful letters. I had played the sleuth and had forgotten my real mission. Again, the flames and a

complete rewrite. (I consider the mission still un-
fulfilled; no one will ever do justice to those letters.)

Then the idea came to me that after all I'd better start
with people, not with "influences." And here all three
volumes of those warm, loving, marvelous letters rose
up in my consciousness as one. She may have been
what we call a recluse, but she kept in vital touch
throughout her life with all the people she loved and
with many who just interested her. (The three volumes
of letters represent only about a tenth of what we know
she wrote.) She was a *people* person. Never mind that
poem about selecting her own society and shutting the
valves of her attention like a stone; her life revolved
around people.

Then I thought of Henry James's notion of reflectors—how, in a work of fiction, the character of the
central figure, say Hamlet, is defined not only by what
he does and what he says, as in his soliloquies, but by
his relations with all the other people in the play,
Claudius and Gertrude, Horatio, Ophelia, Laertes,
Polonius, even Rosencrantz and Guildenstern, and of
course by the largest "reflector" of all, the "prison"
called Denmark.

Was there a structure here? My heart leapt up. So I
said, "Let's start with grandfather." A remote reflector,
maybe—he died when Emily was seven. But the idea
took hold. I couldn't wait to see how it worked. Grand-

father, Samuel Fowler Dickinson, known around town as Squire Fowler, not only worked; he turned out to be a gold mine, or so he seemed to a novice biographer looking for clues. There were many: postrevolutionary America, with just a touch of Tom Paine and deism; New England Puritanism, all austerity and purpose; the town of Amherst, beyond the boundaries of which no Dickinson, Squire Fowler especially, was ever completely happy; Amherst College, for which Fowler sacrificed his fortune and his health, a true martyr. Here were clues aplenty to that rare breed, the species Dickinson. As far as we know, Emily was not one to be curious about her ancestors, much less brood about them; so she may not have known how much of Samuel Fowler there was in her. There was a lot.

But there were no clues to the poetry. Here was the toughest problem of all. Where did that extraordinary talent come from? As I cruised through the ancestry and the immediate family—each a "reflector"—I found little that foreshadowed or paralleled it. Not even a poetical aunt or a musical great-grandmother. Her father and her brother Austin were well-trained lawyers; they wrote decent prose, sometimes with a bit of flavor in it. Austin was the closest to her in temperament and tastes. He had an interior life something like hers, and he loved nature and art. But his letters, compared with Emily's, are, if you're looking for signs of the poet, as water unto wine. He came nowhere near understanding her poetry and its large significance. If he had, he would have done something about it. Sister "Vinnie," Lavinia, three years her junior, may not have understood much; but, to her eternal credit, after Emily died she acted. She got Mabel Todd to prepare some of the poetry for publication. (Emily died in 1886. The "First Series"—116 poems—was published in 1890.)

Most remarkable of all, none of the elders in the family—father, mother, uncles, aunts—seemed to be aware that there was a genius in their midst. One of Emily's remarks about her father sums it up: "My father seems to me often the oldest and the oddest sort of a foreigner. Sometimes I say something and he stares in a curious sort of bewilderment, though I speak a thought quite as old as his daughter." Later she wrote to Thomas Wentworth Higginson: "All men say 'What?' to me" (i.e., What do you mean?). No wonder she talked so much to herself—in her poems. She was the only one around who could understand what she was saying.

And yet, I insist, she was a people person. Just read those letters. Apparently the kind of intimate, personal, face-to-face relationships that she found difficult to achieve (for whatever reason) in everyday living she joyfully established through correspondence. In fact, she seems to have preferred letters, because in them she could convey the essence, the thing itself, love, concern, the joy of life, the fun of cheerful repartee, with none of the distractions of time, space, matter, illness, fatigue, embarrassment, or whatever.

Here's what she wrote a friend about letters: "A Letter always seemed to me like Immortality, for is it not the Mind alone, without corporeal friend?" If more often than not she opted for the mind alone, it was not for want of love. "I know I love my friends," she wrote in her early forties. "I feel it far in here where neither blue nor black eye goes, and fingers cannot reach. I know 'tis love for them that sets the blister in my throat, many a time of day when winds go sweeter than their wont. Or a different cloud puts my brain from home." That was to her Norcross cousins, younger than she by many years, whom she loved as if they were her own children. Such is not the spirit of a recluse.

For better or for worse, to get back to this matter of structure, it seemed to me that I had found it. It had taken five years of trial and error. Even my forbearing wife was finding it hard to understand. Five years later she was beginning to wonder. "Look," she said, "you've been at this ten years and you haven't even got her born yet." I couldn't blame her—Emily doesn't get born until Chapter One of Volume 2. But by then I figured that readers would be ready to hear the cry of the newborn baby breaking the winter stillness. They'd know where this baby came from, what she was being born into and some of the stresses and strains that lay in wait. Some important reflectors had been set up and put to work. She was in context. In justification I quoted Goethe: "Nothing in nature is isolated. Nothing is without reference to something else. Nothing achieves meaning apart from that which neighbors it." Genevieve Taggard had said pretty much the same thing in 1930: "What has been called mystery is character. And character is the key to this extraordinary story —Dickinson family character and Emily's, under the pressure, the light and shade, of the moral climate of Amherst." So, with Goethe and Henry James and Genevieve Taggard on my side, I felt safe.

So on I went, reflector after reflector, searching for clues: early friendships; Amherst Academy, Mary Lyon and Mount Holyoke; a second chapter on Austin, now brought close to Emily; the major friendships of her maturity: Wadsworth, Bowles, Higginson, Helen Hunt Jackson (the author of *Ramona*), Dr. and Mrs. Holland of Springfield (he had been Samuel Bowles's associate on the *Springfield Republican*), the Norcross cousins, and, finally, Judge Otis Phillips Lord of Salem. Each of these people reflected a particular facet, a new light. Each illuminated, in part, the central mystery.

But there was an important reflector still to come. She herself made the suggestion when she wrote in a letter to her friend Joseph Lyman of "the dearest ones of time, the strongest friends of the soul—BOOKS."

(Hence the next-to-last chapter in my *Life*, "Books and Reading.") Again, I had to be selective. I started with the enthusiasms of her youth: Ik Marvel's *Reveries of a Bachelor* and Longfellow's *Kavanagh* (second-rate, no doubt, but, to her, curiously liberating); then on to more powerful stuff, Thomas à Kempis, the Bible, Shakespeare. (You needn't worry about her taste. "While Shakespeare remains," she wrote Higginson, "Literature is firm.") At least the chapter was a passing bow to that false start I had consigned to the flames, the one on literary origins and affinities. It is a large subject; she read widely and had a prehensile memory. The reading list, incidentally, is being steadily expanded by subsequent investigators.

Was this the end? I asked. Something still seemed to be missing. Again Jay Leyda came to the rescue, not only with the idea but with the title of the final chapter, "The Poet." It turned out to be, quite simply, a layman's answer to the question that the chapter begins with: "Just how good is she?" Answer: very good, and here are a few reasons.

Genevieve Taggard was too confident, I think, in suggesting that the mystery of Emily Dickinson was solvable through character. It's good to know all we can about the Dickinsons and the moral climate of Amherst, but the mystery remains. I'm still searching for her, and I'm frank to admit it. Since the mid-1960s the essays, the monographs, the books about Emily Dickinson have come out in a steady stream. What bothers me is the confidence with which many of them pronounce the search to be over: she was *this* or *that*—a lesbian, a psychotic (or at least a neurotic); she was oedipal; she was in love with her brother; she was a repressed feminist—her "rage" shows through in poem after poem; she was a poet in the Meditative tradition; she was a heuristic poet; she was a mystic; she was *not* a mystic; and so on. The attempts to categorize her seem endless. It used to drive Mrs. Bingham crazy. "They all think they own her," she fairly shouted.

Three years ago, during a two-day Emily Dickinson festival in Amherst, at which some of these views were aired, the poet Susan Snively introduced the final session with a word admitting her own confusion. She said, "I feel like the master of ceremonies on the TV show *What's My Line?*" when he comes to the pay-off question, 'Will the real Emily Dickinson please stand up?' "

In conclusion: nobody owns Emily Dickinson or ever will own her. Susan Snively's question is still pertinent. Every honest biographer knows how impossible a definitive biography is of almost anyone, and how completely impossible it is with someone like Emily Dickinson. One thinks of what Matthew Arnold wrote about Shakespeare:

Others abide our question. Thou art free.
We ask and ask. Thou smilest and art still,
Out-topping knowledge . . .

One final anecdote. After I had finished the chapter
on Dr. and Mrs. Holland, I sent it to Mrs. Theodora
Ward, their granddaughter. Mrs. Ward was then living
in Williamstown, Massachusetts. I wanted to get her
approval of the chapter, at least as to matters of fact. In
my opening paragraph I had referred to the legend in
the Holland family that for years Mrs. Holland had
forwarded Emily Dickinson's letters to the Reverend
Charles Wadsworth of Philadelphia. Within a few days
a disturbed telephone call came from Williamstown.
Mrs. Ward had liked the chapter but she was worried
about that legend concerning the letters to Wadsworth.
"There was no such legend," she said. After a bit of
fumbling for the place, I read to her this sentence from
her own book, *Emily Dickinson's Letters to Dr. and Mrs.
Josiah Gilbert Holland* (1951), page 106: "It has always
been understood by the Holland family that for many
years Emily made a practice of sending to Mrs. Holland the letters she wrote to Dr. Wadsworth to be
addressed and forwarded to Philadelphia." I could hear
Mrs. Ward gasp over the phone. "How could I have
said that?" she said. "I must have made it up." (I
thought of Mrs. Bingham's making Edward Dickinson

[84

valedictorian of his class at Yale.) Then, after exchanging with her a few consoling words on the inscrutability of human affairs, I said, "So she's still a mystery, isn't she?" "Yes," she answered (and I'll let Mrs. Ward have the last word), "and I hope she always will be."

On second thought, I'm going to let Emily Dickinson have the last word. The trouble with all this talk about writing the biography—what and how and when and why—is that we tend to forget the fact that she was a poet. I like what E. B. White said about Thoreau: he wasn't a hermit, really, and, professionally speaking, he wasn't much of a naturalist. *"He was a writer, is what he was."* So let's dismiss the notion that she was the Queen Recluse, the Frustrated Lover, the Moth of Amherst. She was a poet, is what she was. I want to leave you with a poem.

People ask me what poem I like best. There are dozens that set the blood coursing through the veins. There are the sad ones, the anguished ones, the terrifying ones; the ecstatic, the joyful, the worshipful; the skeptical, the satiric, the blasphemous; the hopeful and the despairing (often on successive pages). Here's one that is hard to categorize, although, if pressed, I'd be inclined to call it Orphic—after Orpheus, who played the lyre so well that the stones on Olympus took on life when they heard him and the damned in hell forgot their torments when he went there to fetch Eurydice out. The poem is nothing more than a reminder to listen more carefully to the sound of the wind in the trees, but the music of it might be Orpheus's own.

> Of all the Sounds despatched abroad,
> There's not a Charge to me
> Like that old measure in the Boughs—
> That phraseless Melody—
> The Wind does—working like a Hand,
> Whose fingers Comb the Sky—
> Then quiver down—with tufts of Tune—
> Permitted Gods, and me—
>
> Inheritance, it is, to us—
> Beyond the Art to Earn—
> Beyond the trait to take away
> By Robber, since the Gain
> Is gotten not of fingers—
> And inner than the Bone—
> Hid golden, for the whole of Days,
> And even in the Urn,
> I cannot vouch the merry Dust
> Do not arise and Play
> In some odd fashion of its own,
> Some quainter Holiday,
> When Winds go round and round in Bands—
> And thrum upon the door,
> And Birds take places, overhead,
> To bear them Orchestra.

I crave Him grace of Summer Boughs,
If such an Outcast be—
Who never heard that fleshless Chant—
Rise—solemn—on the Tree,
As if some Caravan of Sound
Off Deserts, in the Sky,
Had parted Rank,
Then knit, and swept—
In Seamless Company—

———

Q. I gather you have obtained a tremendous amount of information from Mrs. Bingham's archive, especially from the correspondence between Austin Dickinson and Mabel Loomis Todd. Did you get from those letters any new light on Emily, any new aspect of her character?

A. One of the sad facts about the Austin-Mabel letters is that they have so little to say about Austin's remarkable sister. It is clear that Emily knew about the affair. Once, during Mabel's absence from Amherst, Austin wrote Mabel about his daily visits with Emily: "The conversation is always about you." That Emily tolerated his visits indicates, I think, that her sympathies were with him. A legend has come down that, when asked about the affair, she replied, "I always respected real feeling."

Q. Can you talk about the limits and ethics of conjecture in the writing of biography?

A. I have nothing against conjecture as long as the biographer makes clear that it *is* conjecture. The temptation is to fictionalize—to impute motives that can't be documented, to dress up a scene or a character or an episode with details that might work in a novel but have no basis in fact (e.g., "As Emily stood looking out the window, a tear ran down her cheek.").

Q. Can you give an example in your work of where you made a leap of faith yourself?

A. I suppose every explication of one of her difficult poems is, in a sense, an act of faith—that is, "This is what it means to *me.*" But in general I tried to stick to things that she said and to what people said about her. I was uneasy when I got too far from the documents, and I tried to present the material so that readers could make up their own minds about it without prodding from me. Complete objectivity is of course impossible; all you can do is try your best not to write your own biography in the process of writing someone else's.

Q. Could you tell us something about Emily's letters? Did she ever imagine that they would be published? How were they collected?

A. Here we owe an immense debt to Mabel Loomis Todd. After—or perhaps during—her work on the editing of the poems she began to realize how important the letters were. Fortunately, many of Emily's friends kept her letters, and Mrs. Todd made many solicitations. In the early 1890s she lectured extensively on

[88

Emily Dickinson and let her interest be known. (At the end of one lecture a little lady in black, Abiah Root, committed her priceless collection to the project.) But in several instances Mrs. Todd was too late: the Dickinson letters had been burned; such was the custom in those days. I have a notion, however, that there are letters still around, waiting to be turned up in attics here and there.

My own experience was one of the happiest. One of my students (this was in the late 1950s) told me of a box of letters in his father's house in Charlestown, New Hampshire. They comprised the archive of a man named Joseph Lyman, who was my student's great-grandfather. Would I be interested? Joseph Lyman had been a close friend of Austin's and a visitor for several months in the Dickinson household during the mid-1840s. In due course the box revealed its secrets: a new phase of Emily's life in the Homestead, Vinnie's love affair with Joseph, and seven passages that Joseph had copied from Emily's letters to him. It was a rare find indeed. But not unique. Jay Leyda, following a clue, found a letter of Emily Dickinson's in (if I remember correctly) a book of sermons in the Northampton Library.

So the search should go on—the search for letters (remember that the thousand-odd letters in the Harvard *Letters* are only a small fraction of what we know she wrote) and the search for Emily Dickinson, as I used the word metaphorically in my title. When the *Poems* and *Letters* appeared in the mid-1950s it was as if America had gained a great new cultural resource. The studies that followed—scores of them—are bringing us closer to understanding it. That search, I predict, will never end. She is inexhaustible.

PAUL C. NAGEL

The Adams Women

This evening I want to talk about several aspects of biography, mostly in context of the writing I'm doing now. Perhaps there's no better way to begin than to give you a report on my current work, which takes us to the White House in 1825, when John Quincy Adams was President. I've discovered that his wife, Louisa Catherine Johnson Adams, considered herself a prisoner in the President's mansion—sentenced, as she put it, to do little more than write, while her husband enjoyed the political excitement from which women were then banned. Her relegation to this outsider's role distressed the First Lady, prompting her to express sentiments that say a great deal about women in nineteenth-century America.

Because the lives of women in the early republic are now my interest, let me first show you how much can be learned from the "scribblings" of Louisa Catherine Adams. Her writings took the form of journal entries, letters, poems and drama. One excerpt from Louisa's journal finds her admiring the letters of her late mother-in-law, Abigail Adams. If Abigail's letters should somehow be published, Louisa prophesied, they would "gladden the hearts of many a timid female whose rays too feebly shine. Not for want of merit. But for want of confidence in their powers, and encouragement in the exercise of those capacities with which the almighty has gifted them. Many of the Sex might thus redeem the reputation to which it is entitled. And by proving themselves equal to Mrs. Adams, to practice all the virtuous and feminine duties, convince mankind that the native female mind, clear, full and vigorous in its perceptions, is as capable of solid attainment and enlarged improvement as that of man."

Louisa knew that Abigail had experienced her own kind of distress when she lived briefly in the White House during the winter of 1800–01. Having watched the nation reject John Adams and put the Jeffersonians in power after an alarmingly emotional campaign, Abigail was convinced that the presidential canvas of 1800 was the last for the new republic. Angered and alarmed by the public's vulnerability to what she considered wild demagoguery, she found time in the White House to predict the failure of democracy in America. In her own way Abigail was as unhappy in Washington as her daughter-in-law would be a quarter-century later.

Louisa Adams even wrote bitter plays while she endured her White House captivity. There was one, for instance, called *Suspicion, or Persecuted Innocence,* which contained these lines: "Men ever dread the weakness of our softer sex, but 'tis in the hour of peril that woman displays the energy of her nature and proves herself the noble helpmate of creation's lord." The word *helpmate* intrigued Louisa, who, when she was still in the White House, wrote: "Man's interpretation of the word 'helpmate' as used in the Bible means this: Women made to cook his dinner, wash his clothes, gratify his sensual appetites, and thank him and love him for permission to drudge through life at the mercy of his caprices. Is this the interpretation intended by the Creator, the father of all mercy?" A deeply religious person herself, she often thought about the prevailing notion that heaped guilt and inferiority only on women because of Eve and the apple. As Louisa wrote, "The curse of pain in childbirth and the cares attendant in the rearing of wayward children, this was the punishment annexed to her fault." Because of this atonement, Louisa believed that women didn't deserve "the undermining scorn of her companion who deliberately partook of her sin while he is said to have possessed the Master Mind."

I should also point out that this wife of President
John Quincy Adams had nothing but scorn for politics
and for public plaudits—and particularly for people,
like her husband, who took them so seriously. Even so,
she had the wit to see the ironic role that politics played
in a world that made public life another male advantage. "As the chill of age approaches, love ceases,"
Louisa lamented. Women were left to draw comfort
and gratification from respectability, hoping that "the
fervor of her passions may sleep." A man, however,
could be "the creature of his passions until his death,
thanks to the outlets of politics, ambition and avarice."
"Perhaps," Louisa wryly noted, it was proper to claim
that woman was more "susceptible of what constitutes
the greatness of moral perfection" because her role kept
her above the "ephemeral pursuits of political life."

By opening this talk with the spirited observations of
Louisa Catherine Adams, I certainly haven't concealed
what is my present interest as a biographer. I want to
recapture some lives and outlooks of American women
during the nineteenth century, when the place of the
female in society changed significantly, amid much
controversy. In the manuscripts left by Mrs. John
Quincy Adams and other women in the Adams family,
the biographer has an inexhaustible mine of insight
about some of America's most interesting women, who

lived a hundred or more years ago. Let me illustrate that by returning to Louisa Adams for a moment.

Louisa is one of the most appealing Adams women, and her life has the stuff that makes for bewitching biography. Her sense of loneliness in the White House is itself a good biographical gambit. How could a woman be thus reduced to scribble furiously in the mansion? Louisa was largely bereft of husbandly attentions and had a great deal of difficulty with the menopause. And there were many other troubles during her term as First Lady that add to the fascination of her biography. For instance, she had opened her heart and her home to a niece and two nephews who were the orphans of her elder sister. After she took these young adults with her to the White House she discovered that the two nephews were relishing the physical charms of her personal maid—one at a time, while the other stood guard. Louisa's impulse was to throw the nephews out of the house, but her belief that such behavior was unfortunately normal for most males spared them— although Louisa never forgave them. Meanwhile the niece spent her time in the White House practicing the seductive arts with the President's sons—her cousins— one after another.

Louisa's greatest annoyance as a woman and as mistress of the White House was that the President of the United States rarely consulted her or obeyed her wishes. This was particularly true of his determination to swim in the Potomac. During one such expedition someone rushed to the White House shouting, "The President has drowned!" John Quincy Adams and his valet, Anthony Guista, had been swimming in midstream when their boat capsized, leaving the two men splashing in the nude, their clothes having floated away when the boat overturned. A pair of pantaloons was rescued by the President, who swam to shore unnoticed, leaving passersby to see the boat drifting upside down. This started a rumor which, in an age without television and radio, spread with amazing speed across the country: "President Adams was dead by drowning!" Meanwhile the President and his major domo took counsel together under the bushes along the Potomac. J. Q. Adams ordered the hapless Anthony to don the wet pantaloons and dash to the White House to fetch dry clothes for the President. So away the valet went, dressed in sodden pantaloons that were hardly his size. Spectators, of course, assumed that he was the bearer of bad tidings for the First Lady. Once Louisa realized that her husband was safe, she called the episode "altogether ridiculous." But her hope that it would persuade the President to abandon river swimming was disappointed. J. Q. Adams continued to frolic there, leaving Louisa to ponder further evidence of male folly.

Eventually Anthony Guista, the valet, had his moment of triumph. He prospered in later years, opening a tavern and a small hotel in Washington. When ex-President and Mrs. Adams returned to the city, Adams was a congressman and was virtually bankrupt, and he tried to borrow money from his former servant. Anthony refused. He was as aware of Adams's spendthrift ways as Mrs. Adams was.

During her White House days Louisa became so distressed one summer that she fled Washington, taking off on her own and roaming up and down the Hudson River valley and into Vermont. As some might say today, she was trying to find herself. Yet it is hard to believe that this same Louisa Adams, early in 1815, had traveled from St. Petersburg to Paris with a drunken coachman, a tiny son and a maid who soon ran away in fear. The maid could hardly be blamed—the trip took place in the last days of the Napoleonic Wars, and Louisa had to contend with corpses rotting on the roadside and undisciplined troops challenging her. An astounding woman, this Louisa Catherine Adams, when she felt that circumstances looked to her for direction. Small wonder she was infuriated at the way her husband condescended to her or ignored her.

These glimpses of the life and attitude of Louisa Catherine Adams, perhaps our most fascinating First Lady, will help you to understand why I'm thrilled to be working on a biography of a group of women whose common bond is that they were either born an Adams or married an Adams. My book is tentatively called *Abigail and Louisa: First Ladies and Other Memorable Adams Women,* and it's developing as a series of biographical portraits, linked by a story line extending from 1789 to 1852. The most famous figure, of course, is Abigail Adams, about whom so much has been written, but whom I shall approach from the vantage of her relationship with her two sisters, who were as able and interesting as she was. These were Mary Cranch and Elizabeth Shaw, who became Elizabeth Peabody. I doubt that in England or America three such amazing sisters grew up together, particularly in a rural parsonage.

As for Louisa Catherine, she must be given a large role, especially for her success as a brilliant observer of the life she was prevented by her gender and her husband from touching. I'll also build some of the story around Louisa's tie with *her* sisters, a large tribe who grew up in England in circumstances so tragically different from Abigail's. The plot will linger over the early suspicion and dislike that divided Louisa and Abigail. This antagonism was eventually overcome by affection between these two First Ladies. Rarely were there more talented people in the White House—male or female. When Nancy Harrod married another of Abigail's sons, Thomas Boylston Adams, she was understandably convinced that she too would be catapulted to fame. Unfortunately, her husband turned out to be a pathetically weak figure, cursed with the family's great burden—alcoholism. And so Nancy's life becomes a deeply moving tale of anguished disappointment.

In a story of many contrasts, I go from Nancy to the richest household in Boston, where Abby Brooks, the wife of Charles Francis Adams, grew up with her sisters. Her daughter would live in an Italian apartment as an expatriated female who left America, outraged at the treatment that women suffered in the United States. I also describe the courageous pilgrimage of a woman with cancer fleeing from a wastrel husband and traveling in horrible pain hundreds of miles to die beside her father. This, as readers of *Descent from Glory* know, was Nabby Adams, the daughter of John and Abigail Adams, whose life and attitudes deserve more complete treatment than they have received.

The backdrops for this biography are as diverse as the characters. They include the White House, the court of the czars, the simple house of a rural Massachusetts pastor, a small New England academy, the American minister's residence in London and a Washington salon, to mention just a few. In an epilogue I take the reader to the crypt in Quincy, Massachusetts, where Louisa Catherine rests next to her husband and Abigail reposes beside John. When I come to these final pilgrimages I may use as a guide another woman from the Adams array—Elizabeth C. Adams, known as Cousin

Lizzie, the daughter of Nancy Harrod and Thomas Boylston Adams. She was a kind of vestal virgin who lived to almost one hundred and into the early part of this century. A granddaughter of John and Abigail Adams, she spent her life tending the fires of family veneration, carefully burning her daddy's papers. One can almost see where and why she destroyed material, so much did she fear the biographer. Examining John Quincy Adams's letter books from the period in which he was trying to bolster his poor brother Tom, it is evident when Lizzie tore out offending or revealing material. Luckily, she couldn't find it all. Still, I come near to weeping when I think of the Adams papers that were deliberately destroyed, and not only by Cousin Lizzie.

I discovered these wonderful women as the unforeseen benefit of my project, a dozen years ago, to write a book about how the men in the Adams family developed and shared ideas—the book that became *Descent from Glory*. Until that point I had written books about intellectual history. Along the way I came to realize that I was more interested in the lives of people than in reconstructing ideas. I had wandered afield for a long spell, having to undertake a little of everything, including running a university, which was very unpleasant. Maybe I was chasing up and down my own Hudson valley, years after Louisa did, trying to discover where I belonged. Eventually I found the Adams family, which leaves me to wonder if biographers require a "call," and whether this is true of other kinds of writers. Probably everyone in this room has said on some occasion, "I'm going to write a novel." All of us, I think, can imagine ourselves as novelists. But how many of you have thought at breakfast, "I'm going to write a biography"? Not many, I think. So it may be that a biographer is born and not made; some people just discover it sooner than others.

I believe, however, that my apprenticeship in both professional life and writing was a useful one, because I struggled with the history of ideas. Looking back now, I find that contemplating the development of ideology is good training for a biographer. After all, the intellectual historian takes an idea and brings it to life, reconstructing its exterior and interior. I tried to do it in my books about the federal Union and about the sense of nationality with which Americans were burdened in the nineteenth century. I even wrote a book on the meaning of being from Missouri, where I grew up. For me, working with ideas like these establishes an inviting bridge into the mind and then into the life of people who have held those ideas.

So I crossed that bridge in 1973. I'd had enough of university administration and had also just finished *This Sacred Trust,* the book about American nationalism. In a major change of career and philosophy, I decided to spend most of my time thereafter writing about the lives of people. Since then I've come to appreciate that doing biography is as much an artistic calling as struggling with ideas. The biographer and the intellectual historian are both authors who must rely on the reader. In a good biography readers must be coaxed to see many features for themselves—points that perhaps the writer doesn't care to emphasize. Even mentioning them would appear to belabor; but, left implicit, these insights become an exciting discovery for the reader.

I feel strongly that in biography the author, like a painter, should lead the reader or viewer into a life, and at certain points leave the reader to reflect about what the story means. One of the great joys of biography is that if it succeeds, the author and the reader have each contributed to understanding some of the universals that are implicit in every life. The struggle between good and evil, for instance, is at the heart of the biographical drama, but it is necessarily so delicate and touching that many readers are chilled by the social-scientific treatment of it. Consequently I reject psychobiography as too heavy-handed. Biography in its great moments, long ago and now, has never ignored the mind and motive of the subject.

I'm sometimes asked how I chose the Adamses as a subject. By 1973 I had learned one thing about myself —that I'm an efficient fellow, rather compulsive in

some ways. I knew that writing can be a tedious, exhausting occupation, particularly in biography, where
a lot of research is required, including travel to find the
letters, diaries and other necessary documents. I therefore remembered with interest, as I cast about for a
choice, that the Adams family papers had recently been
opened after being sealed for fifty years. These manuscripts, which ranged from the early eighteenth century through 1889, had been given by present-day
Adamses to the American people. Not only were these
many family manuscripts available in one place, the
Massachusetts Historical Society in Boston; they had
also been filmed and distributed around the nation, so
that biographers could readily use them. It struck me
as a perfect solution for a writer who had lost much
time before turning to biography. The efficient means
of using the Adams sources was, I admit, the major
reason I first looked to the Adamses as a subject.

Of course I had run up against Adamses in my earlier
work. They're hard to avoid in American history. A
little girl in New England is said to have observed to
her father when he asked her how her studies in history
were going, "Daddy, it's fine. But I keep running into
a family named Adams." There's much truth to that.

In launching what I first saw as a book about how
the Adamses shared ideas, I found that it might not be
quite so simple a venture, in time and travel. True, the
papers had been filmed, but the famous diaries and

letters, taking up 608 reels of microfilm, reached only to 1889, leaving a mass of unfilmed material to be read if I wanted to follow the story to the deaths of Henry and Brooks Adams, in 1918 and 1927. And I felt it was essential to do so, since these members of the fourth generation represented quite a contrast to the family at its beginning. Most of Henry and Brooks Adams's papers were in Boston, and I was then living in Missouri. But with a little sabbatical leave time, these challenges of travel and mountainous sources diminished.

Beginning to read the Adams papers film, I hoped that my work as an intellectual historian would have another use. A student of ideology who deals with a broad spectrum of thought has to learn to scan a great deal of material. In my case, for example, that material once included many Fourth of July orations; in fact, I devoted one whole summer to reading Fourth of July orations in the rare book room of the Library of Congress. Without this experience I suppose I might have been intimidated by the massive bulk of the Adams manuscripts and turned instead to the Lee family, whose legacy in source material is of manageable proportions. Soon, however, nothing would have made me back away from the Adamses when I realized that a family biography was what I wanted to do, not a book about family intellect.

My preliminary browsing in the Adams papers had disclosed how wonderfully candid the Adamses—both men and women—were with themselves and usually with each other. It seemed to me to offer an unrivaled opportunity to write about how a remarkable family lived and suffered and loved, which is how *Descent from Glory* came to be, the family pictured at home. Thus a group biography of considerable complexity was begun, ironically, from my desire to approach a book in a tidy, efficient manner. Beyond that, I had no idea at the outset where my choice would eventually lead me, nor that I would come to feel so much sympathy, admiration and identity for and with the Adamses.

When the Adams family biography was finished I turned, as I said earlier, to the Adams women. Curiously, the theme of this new book has taken little character from the fact that these women happened to be members of a famous public family; the Adams women are interesting people in themselves and are very different from each other, as the contrast between Abigail and Henry's wife, Clover, attests. We probably owe the innumerable letters and journals they left to their need to write out of self-defense. Here, possibly, was the only characteristic they shared with their men.

One reason I prize the opportunity of writing this book is that these women recorded so well the outlook and experience of women in that era. Their disclosures are so richly revealing, so helpful in bringing us to understand the story of women in the nineteenth century, as to be unmatched in value and charm. I should also mention that many readers wrote to me after *Descent from Glory* was published, urging me to tell more about the book's various women. An author doesn't have to hear that kind of clarion call very often before being convinced. I want to stress, therefore, that this undertaking isn't inspired by any fad. Actually, I think that the study of women is no longer faddish; the life of women has become a dynamic and increasingly important subject to historical and biographical writing.

My enthusiasm for this latest biographical enterprise is such that when I finish with the Adams women, sometime late in 1986, I'll turn immediately to another group of females—women who, over several generations, were part of the Lee family. Curiously, in 1776 few Americans had heard of the Adams family. At that time the most prominent family in the new republic was the Lee family of Virginia. I've looked into the story enough to know that the Lee women were extraordinary, deserving of a full biographical portrait. And there aren't 608 reels of Lee family papers!

I've been asked whether a man can write a book about women that will be accepted by all sides. In my case, I hope the path by which I arrived at the subject gives me credence. In *Descent from Glory* I revealed how wholly the Adams males depended on their partnership with women. John Quincy Adams was the chief exception. John and Abigail Adams are much together in our minds as the partners they surely were, like salt and pepper. Charles Francis Adams, as he was always willing to admit, would never have succeeded as a writer, as a parent, as a diplomat, if it hadn't been for his wife, Abby Brooks. Henry Adams and Brooks Adams, the brilliant brothers, married remarkable women who were essential partners with their husbands before these wives became gravely ill mentally. The important point is that Adams men, portrayed in their family setting, led me to appreciate the power of their partners—whom I'm now writing about as women facing what life meant and did to females.

Let's return for a moment to the idea of marital partnership. Probably the most successful marriage known to American history was that of John Adams and Abigail Smith. We have all heard something about it, especially about Abigail's courage during the Revolutionary War. But studying Abigail for this biography suggests to me that her marriage was not unique. Abigail was one of many people who believed that male and female were designed by God each to play a very different part in Creation—roles that necessarily sustained and complemented each other. As a result, Abigail's type of union with John Adams was familiar to the eighteenth century, when society, by our measures, was sweetly simple. Home was the center, with mates working in and around the domestic circle; public service usually didn't take husbands away from wives. It was therefore no casual assertion when John and Abigail referred to each other as "my partner." Married folks in the colonial period usually talked of their mates in this way and meant what they said—marriage was a partnership in every respect. Woman and man collaborated in rearing the children and making the hard economic and social decisions.

Abigail Adams is the person who could best summarize the spirit behind this arrangement. She did so in a letter to her sister Elizabeth, which I recently uncovered in the Library of Congress. Writing while she was America's First Lady, Abigail said: "I will never consent to have our sex considered in an inferior point of light. Let each planet shine in their own orbit. God and nature designed it so. If man is lord, woman is *lordess*. That is what I contend for, and if a woman does not hold the reigns of government, I see no reason for her not judging how they are conducted."

If it's true that many men and women of Abigail's generation saw themselves as different but equal partners, the question arises whether marriage—through the nineteenth century and into our own era—has been deteriorating rather than evolving. Obviously it's different now—just look at the partnerships! But are these partnerships, seen through logic and nature, an improvement? The point that Abigail Adams was advocating when she urged John to "remember the ladies" was that females must be held in mind as different but equal. Women were the nurturers and healers

—assignments of the highest order in nature and society. For the Adams women, independent as they were, it was inconceivable for the nurturer also to be a lawyer, and for the partners to march off together after breakfast to their respective professional offices. Abigail Adams foresaw many evils that have come to rule us in the 1980s, and I suspect that she would scoff at our claims of progress. Similarly, I think that the terror, the rapes, and the basic physical and spiritual poverty of our time would be attributed by Abigail and her sisters, and by Louisa, largely to our distorting of the marriage partnership and forsaking the religious faith that helped sustain it. So much more pathetic, then, is the yearning of Mrs. John Quincy Adams to have the same sort of marital partnership that had prevailed between her parents and also between her husband's parents— but which, ironically, Abigail's son denied to his own wife.

With such vivid colors in this group portrait of Adams women, I marvel at what I may find when I write a biography of the Lee women. They, too, were partners in an astounding family across several generations of American history. Their papers repose in the Virginia Historical Society, as the Adams manuscripts do at the Massachusetts Historical Society. Not everyone here may remember that the Lees were powers in our republic well before General Robert E. Lee's time.

Lees were much admired in 1776 by a Massachusetts attorney named John Adams. These famous Lees had wives whose biographies should be written.

Before her marriage, for example, Mrs. Robert E. Lee was Mary Custis, the great-granddaughter of Martha Washington. Mrs. Lee's ideas about marriage and partnership are likely to be revealing and useful, for, despite a life burdened by illness, she produced seven children, of whom four were girls, none ever marrying. A vivid glimpse of these women is now available, for the University of North Carolina Press recently published the charming girlhood diary of one of these daughters, Agnes Lee. The failure of Agnes and her sisters to enter marital partnerships is only one intriguing feature of the lives of the Lee women, stretching back to one who, though widowed, lived happily with a second mate, abjuring marriage for the practical reason that matrimony would force her to surrender her first husband's legacy.

After telling the story of these Lee women I plan to write about the Lees as a family, although my approach is still uncertain. My biography of the Adams family, *Descent from Glory,* has a title that is provocative in its ambiguity. That title, by the way, was someone else's invention, and it has not wholly pleased present-day members of the Adams family, some of whom feel that it's unkind to them. However, in my mind the title does not imply deterioration, but alludes to the experience of being descended from glory. I wonder playfully at times if a biography about the Lees shouldn't be called *Ascent to Glory.* Look what that family managed to achieve! It produced one of the few deities in American history, Robert E. Lee.

General Lee was a very private man, which raises a question that I think every biographer should consider: was Henry Adams right, along with T. S. Eliot and others, when he claimed that modern biography is uncivilized? This charge stemmed from Henry's claim that biography seeks to expose the private scenes of human nature and to hold up for the stares of plain folk the mortality of people who occasionally managed to transcend the ordinary. I wonder how sincere Henry was in this, or how earnest any prominent figure would be in saying that to write biography is only to drag forth the corpse of the subject and display it for the morbidly curious public. Of course, this issue may be obsolete in our era, when all forms of journalism seem bent on complete exposure.

Henry Adams may have denounced biography, but it is worth recalling how, after instructing his intimate friend Elizabeth Cameron to burn the letters they had exchanged, Henry decided at the close of his life that maybe she shouldn't. In reading the seemingly endless diaries of John Quincy Adams or Charles Francis Adams, all so carefully preserved, one might wonder if they were sincere in contending that no other eyes should ever see their journals. J. Q. Adams began his diary when he was just a lad, and he was still dictating entries when he was eighty. He was compulsive about his journal, in the same way that he was devoted to Bible reading and to climbing a hill every morning in Quincy to be sure that the sun rose on time. But his nature brought us one of the greatest diaries of all time, and with it one of the most interesting subjects for a biography—which still begs to be written. I can't believe that J. Q. Adams, Henry Adams or Robert E. Lee, for that matter, would shrink from the modern biographer's searching gaze. One reason for thinking so is that each of these men was aware of the valuable instruction that biography offered to succeeding generations.

Today, however, the biographer is hard-pressed to remain an artist when pitiless scrutiny of public figures is practiced by television cameras morning, noon and night. Both the biographer and the public might well ask: how much disclosure can we witness before we are overcome by trivia, boredom, and poor taste? The question is hard to answer if one believes, as I do, that the reader should have the complete story if a biography is to explain adequately how a life and a personality came and went. To me as a biographer, the dilemma is resolved by the way a story of a life is told—which is to assert, again, that biography is an art. The story should be complete, but it should also be told with affection rather than with ruthlessness, encouraging the readers to peer for themselves into the darkened corner of a life.

I try always to be mindful of this. At home, hanging above my writing desk, are pictures of ten women, each of whom appears in the biography I'm preparing now. I often look up at Abigail, Louisa, Abby or one of the others. These presences, with their gazes upon me a century or more after their time, are moving reminders that the severest requirement imposed on a biographer is humility. Writing about another person's life is an awesome task, so one must proceed with a gentleness born from knowing that the subject and the author share the frailties of human mortality.

———

Q. When you're looking at these diaries, knowing that the authors expected their journal pages to be read, how can a biographer be sure that what appears in the diary is true?

A. Well, you can't. As a writer and teacher I've often contended that our grasp of history (and here I think biography is part of history) must always be incomplete. I've urged graduate students to be content to know that neither they nor their mentors are going to be able to assemble the entire story. Or to feel confident that they've gotten it right.

The Adamses, however, provide more than ordinary assurance. For one thing, they didn't kid themselves;

they were honest about themselves. For another thing, they can be checked by the comments of their brothers, sisters, parents and children. Their papers are so voluminous and observant that one usually follows a clear trail of activity and sentiment. I think the biographer of Adamses can be fairly sure of what to say, because the Adamses often seemed to report on each other's views and doings. They leave the biographer a bit more comfortable.

Even so, there are areas where I have settled for uncertainty. For example, a question that I'm often asked is, were Henry Adams and Elizabeth Cameron lovers in the physical sense? I don't know, although there are those who have been so courageous as to answer that question. While much evidence exists about their relationship, it remains for me impossible to say if their sexual bond was complete. I'm inclined to think it wasn't. Perhaps if more of Henry's journals had survived we could be certain. On a more important point, we can be absolutely sure that Henry Adams did all he could to make Lizzie Cameron a strong, independent person.

Q. Does the emotional fragility, the delicate spirit that the Adamses often manifested, reflect some kind of neurosis?

A. We do know that alcoholism shadowed the family. If we recognized what causes that terrible disease, the biological and emotional roots of it, we might be closer to understanding the Adams family story. It is easier to appreciate that this family was dominated by some of the most extraordinary minds in American history, which played the very dickens with less talented family members who were forced, or felt obliged, to try to keep up. Many Adamses fell by the wayside, as you know, those of you who have read *Descent from Glory*.

Another unnerving burden for Adamses was John Adams's concern for the precarious health of republicanism. From this came his willingness to serve the new nation, though he preferred to be at home, farming and reading. I disagree with those who contend that it was just so much empty rhetoric when John claimed that his heart was at home. I think John left home because of a strong sense of duty. We must remember that the republic was a delicate enterprise in the late eighteenth century, like a flower growing in the second Eden. This concern created a tense household or family atmosphere among the Adamses, to put it mildly. Most affected, perhaps, was John Quincy Adams. Strangely, the founder of this notion, John Adams, was on the whole a wonderfully healthy human being in every sense.

Q. Would you comment on why John Adams and John Quincy Adams both expressed scorn for the average citizen?

A. I haven't found them as contemptuous on this score as the Adamses have usually been described as being. John Adams was especially concerned because he feared that the unlettered citizen was being asked to do more than was prudently possible. The question then was: Should the average citizen be brought into the decisions, the judgments that a republican system entailed? But this question, so vital to the Adams point of view, was a commonplace in the late eighteenth century. Our electoral college was created to keep the choice of a President from becoming a political decision in the hands of a great many people. Out of his misgivings John advocated the system of checks and balances, a cautious division of authority in a republic, which was one of his great contributions to American history. President Adams was impressed by history's sobering lessons. Anyone who reads history, these days especially, should know what a discouraging, distressing view of the human prospect it affords. John Adams and other family members spoke aloud about this more than most people did, and earned wide dislike after the Jeffersonians and Jacksonians began claiming that the typical citizen could succeed at everything.

Q. Please tell us more about why you are now writing a biography about women.

_A._ To begin with, I like and admire women. I found in some thirty years of university teaching that my best students in history by far were women. Now I want to pay respect to a part of our society whose achievements haven't been fairly acknowledged. I'm also enchanted by the story of the Adams women, and by an opportunity to tell it in a way that brings to all of us the rich legacy of their lives and thoughts. From them we can learn much about the ordeal of women generally. Actually, the Adams ladies can represent, as well as speak to, women for all time.

Q. How do you approach the job? Where do you start when you come across 608 reels of film?

A. In the film, which moves day by day, you start at the beginning. The published Adams papers, however, are organized in several groups, and chronologically in each. The letters are in one category, the diaries and journals are in another, and the public papers in a third group. The latter I didn't bother with much. Of course I didn't read all 608 reels—that's where scanning helps. But the most important tactic is to catch the cadence of the documents, sensing when an event or a statement of consequence is approaching. At that point you take your time. Then you hasten on. Sounds very mystical, and it probably is.

Q. Is it difficult reading all that original handwriting?

A. It frequently is, but today not everyone has to tackle the filmed manuscripts. Large portions of the diaries of the Adams men have been edited and printed, as well as some of their private and public papers. These volumes have been published by the Harvard University Press, which has undertaken a project extending well beyond our time. The papers are edited for publication at the Massachusetts Historical Society, where the job has been done with great success.

As for the handwriting, it varies, of course. It becomes especially illegible when Adamses tried to conserve paper by writing first horizontally and then turning the sheet to write vertically. The women were more inclined to do that. But even this style can be read —after you stay with it long enough.

RONALD STEEL

Living with
Walter Lippmann

A biographer and his subject are, as I discovered in writing about Walter Lippmann, both partners and antagonists—at least when the subject of the biography is very much alive and exceedingly interested in the results. They become locked in a contest of undetermined duration, over issues that are always in dispute, for stakes that are never clearly delineated. It's like a marriage. Each is linked to the other for the duration, however long that might be. To break the pact would be an admission of bad faith. Given the divorce rates these days, one could even say it is more binding than most marriages. And for the writer, at least, the financial consequences of a rupture would be so calamitous as to make any kind of cohabitation better than none at all.

In using the marriage analogy I don't want to evoke

images of Strindberg or even Eugene O'Neill. I see it more like a courtship, a contract and a contest, an *agon* of the sort that Balanchine depicts in his ballet. Each partner has his own motives, which are never fully expressed. Each observes a mode of behavior, ruled by strict convention. Each carefully protects himself while realizing that his full development can come only in union with the other.

If the players are antagonists, they are also partners, joined until the force that united them has burned itself out and produced its long desired, perhaps long dreaded, offspring. This does not mean, by the way, that my relationship with Walter Lippmann was contentious or that we were forever wrestling. We could hardly have been more polite and cordial with each other. Walter Lippmann was an immensely courtly man. During the five years I knew him I don't think I ever heard him be impolite or raise his voice in anger. The emotions that he felt were well restrained. Rather, our contest was an unexpressed one. He knew and even accepted, both with resignation and with hope, that in some sense I held his life in my hands. He felt confident that whoever he was and whatever he had done would transcend what I had to say about him. But he also knew that whatever I said couldn't help but have some impact on that intangible reality that we call reputation. By the same token, we both knew that I would be judged by what I wrote about him. And so, here too, we were locked in a mutual endeavor and a mutual anxiety.

I had expected, before I started studying his life and writing about it, to become absorbed in his career, to admire him, to be a privileged observer at the intellectual banquet that covered the first seven decades of the twentieth century. But what I had never expected was the way I would come to fear him. Not to fear anything he might say or do to me, for it was hard to imagine (and increasingly as I came to know him) any way in which he might wish me harm. Rather, I came to fear the way in which he would insidiously take over my life—take it over in time, until I often felt that I hardly had any life outside that of Walter Lippmann, and also by forcing me constantly to define myself in terms of him and him in terms of me. He became, in both a horrible and a fascinating way, a doppelgänger. When confronted with some example of questionable or even outrageous behavior on his part I found myself asking how I would have behaved in those circumstances. Would I have been more feeling, more noble, more honest? What right did I have to judge him? How could I ever know enough to do so? In judging his behavior, in watching him react to an event, in reading his cool columns of analysis, was I really putting myself in that place instead of dispassionately viewing him?

The answer, of course, is yes, I did judge him. I think this is a continuing problem that all biographers face.

In my own case I felt drawn to Lippmann for a great many reasons, not all of them intellectual by any means. And I think I was often severely judgmental of him because I saw so many of his follies and his foibles and his rationalizations and his self-delusions in myself.

I can't say that it was my lifelong ambition to write about Walter Lippmann, even though it did ultimately become the preoccupation of a significant part of my life. The idea came from the late Richard Rovere, the esteemed Washington correspondent of *The New Yorker*, a man with an immense knowledge about affairs of state and with a somewhat bemused detachment from the more distraught affairs of its practitioners. Though I had never met Rovere, I had often read his "Letter from Washington" with great admiration, and I was pleased and surprised to receive a phone call from him one day. "This is Richard Rovere," he said, adding with characteristic diffidence, "I work for *The New Yorker* magazine. I'm working on a project involving Walter Lippmann, and I wonder if you would come down to the Century Club and have lunch with me to talk about it." Well, I accepted immediately, never having been inside the doors of that august institution, nor, of course, having met Rovere, who was so admired by all journalists. I would have gone even if he had asked me to discuss the repair of his air conditioner.

On the appointed day we met. After a certain

amount of hemming and hawing, Rovere, who was a shy man, not at all at ease among strangers, told me he had been engaged by the Atlantic Monthly Press to do a study of Walter Lippmann. That study had begun in an effort to edit Lippmann's letters for publication. Rovere had discovered, first with delight and then with mounting horror, that Lippmann's private papers were far more voluminous than anything he had ever anticipated. They numbered well over fifty thousand, not even counting all his collected columns and manuscripts.

Rovere was naturally appalled by the amount of work that would be involved just going through this correspondence, some of which dealt with the most complicated affairs of state and others with matters like replacing faucets and taking care of his laundry and getting his grass cut. As he went through this vast amount of material, separating the wheat from the chaff, Rovere discovered many things about Lippmann's life that he hadn't known. He was primarily impressed by the degree to which Lippmann had been involved in affairs of state, not merely as a disinterested commentator, but as an active participant in politics. And he realized that to edit the letters would do an injustice to the enormous richness of the material. The only way to deal with it, he concluded, was to do a full-scale biography. And when he made that realization he withdrew, first in caution and then in alarm. It would take too much of his energies away from his magazine column and would dominate his life. So he reached out for some assistance. He asked if I would be interested in collaborating with him.

Well, I was surprised by the invitation and flattered. But cautious, too. If he was alarmed by the amount of work, shouldn't I also be alarmed? Would it consume my life as well? I also feared what it would be like to collaborate with someone. I had never collaborated on a book with anyone before; I wondered if it wouldn't be twice as much labor as doing it oneself. I also wondered whether Rovere, being so much more eminent, would receive the credit and I would end up doing the work. Finally I decided against it.

But Rovere was a persistent man—perhaps out of desperation. So he urged me to reconsider. At another of our lunches at the Century Club he confessed, with an air of great conspiracy, that he would actually like to pull out of the project and turn it over to me. He felt immensely relieved by this confession. He assured me of what a wonderful intellectual adventure the biography would be. He hinted not only of the great excitement I would get from doing it, but of all kinds of commercial rewards that lay down the road.

Well, I was tantalized, I must say. I had recently written a foreign policy book that had been published to some critical acclaim but very little commercial success. The Lippmann project seemed enticing on those grounds. And certainly it was attractive on intellectual grounds. I had long admired Lippmann. I had read his columns since the early 1960s and, like many young journalists, had tried to emulate him. The project would get me deep into the subject of politics and policy formation and public opinion. It would pose a new challenge. And it would get me away from political polemics, which I was beginning to tire of.

Eventually Rovere gently, and with some trepidation, extricated himself from the project and explained to Lippmann that I would be taking over. I was surprised at the ease with which Lippmann agreed, since he hardly knew me. I was surprised at his willingness to let someone who was virtually a total stranger rummage through his private papers and pass judgment on him. What if I distorted the material? What if I passed a judgment on his life that made it unrecognizable? Or unfair? What if I turned out to be malicious or merely inept? What if—worst of all—he died before the book was completed and he therefore had no chance to refute it? The perils on his side were considerable. The dead have no right of redress—the biographer, for better or worse, has the last word. As Oscar Wilde said, "Biography adds to death a new terror."

Despite these dangers, Lippmann was willing to have the book written. He was even mildly enthusiastic. I think he felt a dread about what I might say, mixed with pleasure over the fact that he would be the focus of so much labor. I also think he was immensely self-confident about the significance of his career. I don't think it occurred to him that history, or even his biographer, would find him seriously wanting.

He also established certain controls. On the basic points he was immensely generous. He gave me unrestricted access to his papers, which meant that I could go through everything; nothing was cordoned off from my scrutiny. He also gave me exclusive access to them, which meant that nobody else would be allowed to use the material as long as I was working on the book.

One further question remained to be negotiated. This is a problem that every biographer has with a subject who is still alive. There are great advantages, of course, when the subject is alive, and also a great disadvantage, which is the biographer's lack of complete freedom to say what he wants about the subject. William Manchester's experience with the Kennedy family was still very much in my mind when Lippmann and I were conducting these negotiations. I felt that if I were going to write this book I had to be free to say about Lippmann whatever, in my own best judgment, was correct. I didn't feel that he should be able to veto anything. He, of course, felt that he should have certain power over the final result. There were dangers in giving me *carte blanche.*

Ultimately the dilemma turned out to be more apparent than real. We soon arrived at a rather strange gentlemen's agreement. I would write whatever I felt. Lippmann would read the completed manuscript. If he was unhappy about any part of it he would make his objections known to me. At this point I could reconsider and change whatever he objected to. If I wouldn't, we would submit the parts in question to a three-man board of overseers—one chosen by him, one by me, and one presumably impartial. Lippmann chose his lawyer, Louis Auchincloss, who is also, of course, an eminent novelist; I chose Rovere, and the impartial centrist was Arthur Schlesinger, Jr. They dutifully lent their assent. But we never had to call upon them— because Lippmann, of course, died before the book was finished.

The matter of the publisher was soon settled. Lippmann's old friend, Edward Weeks of the Atlantic Monthly Press, had been his publisher for some years and had actually persuaded him to have his biography done. Lippmann had always resisted writing his own memoirs. He had an abhorrence of the past. He once started an autobiographical fragment and stopped after a morning's work. I think it not only bored him to think about the past; it pained him. Introspection was not something that gave him any great pleasure. His column was called "Today and Tomorrow," and that's what he was preoccupied with. I think that for both intellectual and psychological reasons it was important for him to think that way.

There were no hitches, really. We agreed on the basics—money and that sort of thing. Arthur Schlesinger suggested that I use a literary lawyer to negotiate the contract, and he gave me the name of a very reputable one in Boston. The lawyer negotiated what I thought was a very good contract, and everything went fine until I discovered that the lawyer's wife was an editor at the Atlantic Monthly Press and sat in the office next to Mr. Weeks. I thought this proximity was a little too close, and that it raised a potential conflict of interest. Would this lawyer really fight on my behalf against his wife's boss? I mentioned this and he said, "Oh, don't worry. It happens all the time in Boston. Everybody's related to everybody else. We'd never get any business done in this city if we didn't have to negotiate with one another."

I should explain at this point what was in my mind when I took on this project. As I envisaged my book, it was an intellectual biography—a book about American foreign policy from 1945 on, through the eyes of Walter Lippmann. But as I got into the material, of course, it changed dramatically, and I ended up writing a book of forty-five chapters in which I didn't even get to the Cold War until Chapter Thirty-three. And instead of writing exclusively about foreign policy I found myself writing about the press, literature, philosophy and the arts. And instead of finishing in three years, as my contract firmly stipulated, it took me three times as long. And also, rather than just commenting on what Walter Lippmann did and said and wrote, I found myself delving ever deeper into who he was. What began as an act of exposition increasingly became a detective story, in which Lippmann was both the client and the quarry. There were times, in fact, when I wasn't sure where he left off and I began. And I understood why Rovere had been so eager to lay down this burdensome treasure that he had come across.

Rovere had warned me of some of the shoals. Lippmann, he once hinted, was a much less disinterested observer of politics than he had let on to be. At the time I didn't pay much attention to this. It wasn't until I got much deeper into the research that I uncovered all kinds of involvements that cast a very different light on the ethics of the journalist as observer and the need for the journalist to stand back from his subject. It put a new light both on Lippmann and on the role that journalists play in the formation of public opinion.

I also found that it wasn't enough just to explain what Lippmann said about an issue. My first discovery was that I had to go back way before 1945. I had to deal with that extraordinary life that began as an acolyte to Theodore Roosevelt, as a student of Santayana and William James, as a founder of the *New Republic*, as an aide to Woodrow Wilson and the man who had helped put together Wilson's famous Fourteen Points address outlining a settlement of World War I, and later as editor of the New York *World*, et cetera, et cetera.

And beyond simply explaining that life, which extended far back from the Cold War issues that had originally attracted me, I also had to know who he was. I had to know this because I found myself continuously dealing with material that didn't necessarily make intellectual sense or that was intellectually baffling in one way or another. Why, for example, did he take a particular position rather than another? What were the emotional forces that drove the intellectual discourse? I got the first hint of the reason from Lippmann himself in an offhand remark he made in 1915, when he was only twenty-five, in a review of a book by John Dewey, one of the many, many articles he wrote for the *New Republic*. It was just a grain of sand in the enormous pile of his articles. He wrote: "Philosophies are the very soul of the philosopher projected. And to the discerning critic may tell more about him than he knows about himself. In this sense a man's philosophy is his autobiography. You can read in it the story of his conflict with life."

I thought that was an amazingly revealing statement —and tantalizing, of course. Because Lippmann's own philosophy, the attitude that he brought to issues, explains a great deal about his life. Just to take one example. Some of you may have read his book *A Preface to Morals*, which is about stoicism and what is now disparagingly called secular humanism. The book is a powerful statement. Not very many journalists write books of moral philosophy. But aside from that, I discovered that this book, which was written during the last unhappy years of his first marriage, was also influenced by that marriage. I learned that the position he took stemmed from his unhappiness and that he wouldn't have written the book in that way some years later, during what was a very happy second marriage. So I came to realize that only if I understood him as a person and only if I understood his life could I understand his political positions.

Just as the positions that he took illuminated some of the more mysterious aspects of his personality, peripheral events could also take on considerable significance. I found myself, for example, devoting a great deal of attention to the election of 1924. That was hardly one of the turning points in American history—only a political junkie could tell us today who the three candidates were. But what was interesting was Lippmann's choice. Lippmann had grown up during the Progressive movement and had always supported Progressive candidates. He obviously could not vote for Calvin Coolidge. In that election, however, he chose to support the Wall Street lawyer John W. Davis, who was running on the Democratic ticket, instead of Robert La Follette, the great Progressive from Wisconsin. If you were doing a book of American history you wouldn't devote much space to that. But in a work of biography, that election was far more important to me than the election of 1932 or '36 or '40 or '48, or whatever, because it showed something significant about Lippmann. I had to go into his personality.

Yet I was wary about entering the shoals of psychobiography; I didn't feel competent to psychoanalyze Lippmann. But I also realized that I needed a lot of information—information that I wasn't getting from the printed word. Nobody had ever written a biography of Lippmann. The basic information just never appeared. It wasn't even in his letters. Although Lippmann was a magpie and had accumulated great heaps of letters, all the way back to grammar school, they didn't indicate much, for example, about his family, his emotional involvements, his anxieties. I found that I didn't have a great deal of material that was absolutely essential.

I also realized that he was reluctant to delve into this material. He never volunteered any personal information, and I was hesitant to engage in what he would consider to be prying. So I certainly wasn't going to say, "Why did you divorce your first wife?" or "Why did you turn your back on Woodrow Wilson?" I thought, I'll start out very easy and I'll ask him the world's simplest question. So I said, "Oh, by the way, what was it precisely that your father did for a living?" There was this horrible silence. Lippmann had these very heavy, hooded eyes, and he looked at me for what seemed minutes. Then he said, "I wouldn't want you to make this book a novel." Then he changed the subject. I was absolutely fascinated by this—not so much distressed, because I could easily find out what his father did—but fascinated by his reluctance to talk about it even to that degree.

So what began as a perfunctory question came to assume significance. I had to ask myself, what could this man have been? Was he a drunk? A gangster? A gunrunner? What was so unusual about him that Lippmann didn't want to talk about? It showed his extreme sense of privacy. But also an extreme sensitivity regarding his parents. Well, the episode led me on a search. And I began digging. I soon found that although Lippmann claimed he had no living relatives, there was indeed a cousin. (He had no brothers or sisters, and the parents were dead.) There was a cousin who lived in New York with an immense grudge against Lippmann who was very eager to tell me everything he knew. He had been a neglected cousin and he wasn't particularly successful in life, so you can imagine what a rich trove of information he was—some of which I had to be careful of. But other things—just a description of the family life—were immensely useful to me.

Aside from the cousin, I realized that I was going to have to conduct far more interviews than I had thought. Because it was my first biography, I had gone into it thinking, "I'll get the stuff basically from talking to Lippmann and from the library." But, as I learned, you have to conduct many interviews. Some of these are immensely valuable, some are a total waste of time. I also learned the degree to which people are cautious —particularly older people, his contemporaries, who obviously were more knowledgeable about him, but also less eager to tell me what they knew. I found that there's an unspoken conspiracy among people not to speak badly of one another if the other person is in a position to return the insult. As Stravinsky was quoted as saying, "After eighty all contemporaries are friends." I found that was often the case.

Another disappointment occurred when I tracked down his personal secretaries, who were really his assistants. These are women who had worked very closely with him for many years. I thought, now I'll get the inside story about his relations with all these Presidents and secretaries of state and congressmen. To my surprise, however, one of these women, who worked with him during the 1950s, would never say much more than "Mr. Lippmann was such a wonderful man." She would tell me absolutely nothing. Luckily, another assistant during a later period was a gold mine of information, and I'm immensely grateful to her for insights

into Lippmann's professional life during the Kennedy
and Johnson administrations.

There was one source that seemed the most important of all—and one that I had great difficulty finding.
I knew that Lippmann had been married to the same
woman for twenty years. I knew that he had divorced
her in 1938, that a very messy scandal had ensued, and
that he had soon thereafter married the wife of his best
friend. Naturally he had never spoken of any of this to
me, nor did I feel, from other attempts to elicit information from him, that he would. I felt, however, that I had
to make every effort to find the first wife. I didn't even
know if she was alive. I asked Lippmann. He said he
didn't know. I asked him where she had last been living. He said he didn't know. I asked him where she had
lived right after the divorce. He said he didn't know.
I asked his friends. They said that none of them had
seen her since 1938. The woman simply disappeared.
Eventually I learned that she had remarried. I found
the name of the person she had married and through a
long process of exclusion at last tracked her down. I
found her in the most obvious place, which I should
have thought of all along: in the country house that she
and Lippmann had lived in in the twenties on Long
Island. But that was only the beginning: finding her
was not seeing her. First of all, I wrote her a long, polite
letter explaining who I was and that I was doing this

authorized biography of her first husband. And could I please see her? Since it was going to be unavoidable to mention her in this book, I wanted to get her side of the story of Walter Lippmann. I also explained that this was going to be the only book about Walter Lippmann for some time and how important it was to posterity to get this right.

Well, absolute silence. I wrote another letter. Silence again. Then I tried to call, and I got her second husband on the phone. He said, absolutely not—she won't speak to you. So I started calling at odd hours of the day and night, thinking maybe I'd catch her alone. I was preparing to come knocking on the door when I did catch her by phone, early one morning. She said, "I don't think I could talk to you unless Walter gave his permission." So I screwed up my courage and went to Lippmann and said, "Guess what? I found the first Mrs. Lippmann." And he said, "Oh?" He didn't much seem to care where she was. He probably knew. I said, "I'd like to talk to her." He said, "Well, that's all right." And I said, "But she won't talk to me unless she has your permission." And he said, "Well, what would you like me to do?" And I said, like a child asking his father for a note to the teacher, "Would you please write her a note saying that it's all right with you that I talk to her?" And he said, "All right," and he took out a piece of paper. He had a strange scrawl that was very hard to read, and he addressed a note. But not to her, and not to me, but to some force of nature, saying: "This is to say that I, Walter Lippmann, have no objection if Ronald Steel speaks to Faye Albertson Heatley."

So I sent the note off to her and phoned a few more times, and in due course an appointment was set up for noon. I drove out to Wading River, on the North Shore of Long Island, one February morning, not knowing what to expect. Lippmann had lived a rather grand life, and I expected something grand, perhaps modeled on the houses in Oyster Bay, where the Lippmanns had spent a great deal of time. I pulled into the driveway of a ramshackle house, set back on the edge of a nondescript village. I rang the bell and a housekeeper let me in. The house was furnished with the kind of furniture one sees in yard sales and college dormitories; they obviously didn't have much money. And I dimly saw, shuffling through the kitchen, the husband in his pajamas. He wasn't very receptive. And ignored me. I was led into the living room to meet Mrs. Heatley, the first Mrs. Lippmann.

I still expected someone rather imposing, on the model of Alice Roosevelt Longworth, I suppose. What I found was very surprising. She was sitting there, a woman of about eighty, in a brightly colored floral print dress. She had dyed blond hair, and glasses that sweep up at the edges. The chairs had wide arms of the kind you can set things on. And in her hand she held a tall glass with ice cubes and whiskey in it. She asked me if I would like a highball. I said no, I couldn't handle it at that hour. She was very gracious. And so we sat down and talked.

Well, once I got over my shock I found her really quite a charming lady. But a puzzling one. The puzzle was, what did she and Walter Lippmann have in common? She was not an intellectual woman, and indeed there was no reason why she should be. Nor was she a reflective person, or a particularly perceptive one. I asked her what I thought were the most basic questions about Lippmann. It wasn't that she was being secretive; it was mainly that her mind didn't work that way. She didn't remember most of the people who I thought were important in their lives.

However, she did tell me a few things just in passing that seemed fascinating. She was talking, for instance, about their trips back from Maine in the summers. When they drove through New Hampshire, she said, Walter would always refuse to stay at the grand hotels that were restricted, that discriminated against Jews, even though he could "pass," in her words. She was a very Nordic woman herself. I thought that was interesting because I wouldn't have expected it. She also told me that when they were married they were quite poor. Walter had refused to accept money from his parents, who were quite wealthy, when he discovered that a great deal of his parents' income came from slum tenements. She said that she and Walter had bought their house on borrowed money and had fixed it up themselves. It wasn't until Lippmann became editor of the New York *World* in 1922 that he had any money himself.

But I left feeling as puzzled as when I arrived. Because I didn't understand what it was that had brought these two people together. I felt like the reporter in *Citizen Kane* who finally finds the first wife, a broken-down entertainer in a nightclub, and expects to get the lowdown. But the first Mrs. Lippmann didn't have any grudges, and I was struck by the degree to which she felt charitable and even protective toward him.

Her chance remark about the hotel and the Jews intrigued me, because Lippmann had never himself associated in any way particularly with Jewish causes or organizations, and I think many of his readers would have been surprised to discover that he was Jewish. In assessing this it's important to remember that he grew up in a time very different from our own. There was no reason why he should have made a point of being Jewish. He had been brought up when it was fashionable for young intellectuals to be cosmopolitan. To be ethnic was considered parochial—just the opposite of today. Even Louis Brandeis, before his conversion to Zionism at the time of the First World War, said he wanted to be known not as a Jew but as an American.

Lippmann had grown up in New York as part of

"Our Crowd"—the rich German Jews who looked
with disdain on the Yiddish-speaking immigrants on
the Lower East Side. As one of his gentile friends said
to me, "Walter simply decided that he wasn't Jewish."
Well, maybe, I said. But I learned that that wasn't quite
the case. Also, one simply doesn't decide such things,
as all Jews know. Nor did Lippmann. During the
course of burrowing in the archives I came across a
remarkable series of letters between him and the editor
of a Jewish publication in the 1920s. They pertained to
two articles that he had written on the subject of Jews
in America. And there he had used a startling vocabu-
lary, one that put the blame for anti-Semitism largely
on the Jews themselves. What struck me was the intensity of the view and the exaggeration of the language.
I realized that this was not simply an intellectual subject for him—that being a Jew was not a matter of
indifference. It was something about which he felt very
strongly. For he had expressed himself in this powerful
emotional language.

Until that time I had never intended to write anything about Lippmann and the Jews or the Jewish
issue. He had expressed himself so little on Jewish matters that there seemed no reason to do so. But after that
discovery I began to look at the question more closely
—not only at things he said but at things he didn't say.
I realized that he had ignored issues that one would
have expected him to comment on as America's pre-

mier columnist. He was strikingly quiet, for instance, about the Nazi treatment of the Jews and even about the Holocaust and later about Israel. It was as if he had tried to step back deliberately from discussing such issues. But even then I hadn't fully decided to deal with this until I came across the very strange relationship he had with Felix Frankfurter.

Frankfurter had been his friend since the First World War. They had been together in Woodrow Wilson's administration as young officials in the War Department. There had been intense correspondence between them from that time on. When Lippmann was editor of the *World* and Frankfurter was at Harvard Law School they wrote each other almost every day. Or, I should say, Frankfurter wrote Lippmann every day. Because Frankfurter was an indefatigable letter writer—he probably wrote forty people every day.

And so I went through boxes and boxes of Frankfurter-Lippmann material. Most of it was about political issues, so it was very rich, and I expected to keep going through those boxes until Frankfurter's death—or my own. But suddenly, in 1933, the letters stopped. I was puzzled by that. For no apparent reason, there were just no more.

I asked Lippmann about it, and he said, "Oh, Felix used to bombard me with those letters because he wanted them published in the *World*. And I couldn't publish everything he sent me, so I just stopped writing and he got angry and didn't write me back." So I said, "All right, but you stopped being editor of the *World* in 1931, and the letters continued until 1933." Well, he said, we just stopped writing. I was stymied but didn't know what else to do about that—Frankfurter, of course, was long since dead—until I received a packet of letters from a colleague who was writing about an important figure of the period. One was a letter from Frankfurter to this person explaining that he had broken with Lippmann over a column Lippmann had written in 1933 about Hitler. There was also a letter from Frankfurter to Lippmann saying, in effect, I understand that you claim that you don't understand why I broke with you. Here is the reason I broke with you: I couldn't imagine anybody using such language about the Jews and not being sensitive to what Hitler was doing, et cetera. And there was a letter from Lippmann replying: I can't understand how you thought this. You misunderstood what I meant, et cetera.

It was a very emotional correspondence. Lippmann could hardly *not* have remembered it. So with considerable trepidation I asked him about it. But he just brushed it aside. He said, "I just don't remember that." So it was at that point that I realized that I had to deal with this issue. I hope I didn't put too much emphasis on it. To me it seemed a very significant one in Lippmann's life, not because he was Jewish and therefore had to become involved in Jewish causes, but because it was an issue that aroused his emotions whenever it came to the surface. It was one, I became convinced, that affected his views toward politics and also suffused his personality. In my mind there was no way I could not deal with that question. I only hope I did so in a way that didn't do him an injustice.

One of the things I had to adjust myself to was the different world that Lippmann lived in. He was a person who was used to enormous comfort. He'd grown up rich and comfortable. He took it for granted that he would know the rich and the famous. Once I came across a note scrawled in his engagement book during a trip to Greece in the 1950s: "Saw the king, the prime minister, etcetera, the usual people." And for him they *were* the usual people. For me it required a leap of understanding to inhabit with him a world of such usual people. And I had to assess how that affected his judgment.

Lippmann continued to write his newspaper column regularly until 1967, when he and Helen decided to move to New York, and he wrote a magazine column sporadically after that until 1971. The move to New York was one that puzzled many of their friends: they had lived in Washington for thirty years. But they had left New York in 1938 unwillingly, under the cloud of marital scandal. Both of them were also native New Yorkers, and they had always looked back on New

York as a place that was the center of their world. So when they retired, it seemed like a logical thing to do. Also, the atmosphere in Washington was unpleasant between him and Lyndon Johnson—there was such strong feeling about the Vietnam War at the time.

So they came back. It was the beginning of a very bad period for them. From the time that Lippmann retired, everything went dramatically downhill. I came into their life somewhere around this time. At first, before they decided to live in New York, they thought they would live in Europe. Lippmann had been a great friend of Bernard Berenson, and they thought perhaps they could live in baronial splendor as he had. They went to Florence to look for a villa just like his, like *I Tatti*. They didn't find one, and prices were high and the traffic and noises were awful. They decided that that wasn't going to work.

Next they went to France. They had always been Francophiles, and they bought a lovely old mill outside Fontainebleau. However, the servants were surly and incompetent, and they decided it was too far from Paris. Four weeks later they sold it and moved into a hotel in Paris—the Meurice—and stayed there the rest of the summer and then came back to New York. Then they decided they'd stay in New York after all. So they bought a seventeen-room duplex on Eighty-fifth Street and Park Avenue. Incidentally, if you want to know what prices were in 1967, that seventeen-room duplex cost $125,000. But maintaining the apartment proved more than they could deal with. They sold it a year later—at a great profit, by the way—and moved into an apartment hotel, the Lowell.

The city didn't work for them. It had changed a great deal—it had become dirtier, more crowded, more violent—and they were much older, of course. They never really felt happy here. And Lippmann's own health went steadily downhill. His legs began to give way; he had a heart attack early in 1973, and his memory began to go. That was a very sad thing to watch, because here was someone whose whole life had been one of the mind, who really was not very good at the practical things. Helen had been his great aid in that area. And when his memory went he became very dependent. He lived a little too long, I think, in the sense that everything was collapsing around him.

Helen couldn't stand to watch this disintegration in his health and his mental capacities. She distanced herself from him. It was an extreme reaction on her part; she was much criticized by her friends for her behavior at this time. I think it was a neurotic compulsion on her part. She just couldn't stand the thought of death and decay—it was too personal for her; I think it reminded her too much of her own mortality.

Whatever the reason, she couldn't stand it, so she put him into a nursing home, a very elegant one on Park Avenue, run by a distant relative of William James. He languished there for more than a year. He never complained about it. It was striking to me—how people treated him then: who came to see him, which friends remembered him, and which friends who had always been so eager to see him forgot about him. When you're a famous person and cease to be active—particularly in journalism and politics—when you're no longer a mover or a shaker, the world quickly forgets or is too busy for you. He was there in a kind of isolation.

Once Helen brought him up to Maine. It didn't work. He was aware, of course, of the degree to which he had been shunted off to the nursing home. I never heard him complain about that—to me or to anyone else. But just before he died he said he had a strange dream in which he found Helen in an adulterous relationship. He was very angry, and he told her he would forgive her but would never live with her again. I thought that was so poignant, especially considering how their own relationship had begun.

As I say, it was easy to criticize Helen. But I think she was in the grip of emotions that she herself couldn't comprehend. She was a person many people considered difficult. I got on with her very well. I always wanted to interview her—she was an extremely intelligent and articulate woman; but I kept postponing it because I didn't want to seem to be going behind Lippmann's back, since he was somebody who guarded his privacy so much.

Finally the opportunity came, not at my initiative, but at hers. I got a letter at the end of 1973 saying, "Could you please come by and have tea with me? I want to talk to you. I've come across some remarkable things." So I immediately called her and we set a date, and I came on the appointed day, maybe a week later, at six o'clock in the evening. I found her in her peignoir and her slippers—she had completely forgotten about it and she seemed quite distraught. But she said, "Well, stay anyway. A most amazing thing has happened. I've just received four letters from my first husband's widow." Her first husband, Hamilton Fish Armstrong, had died some months before, and in his estate he left four letters for his first wife, for Helen, with instructions that they be given to her on his death.

They turned out to be letters that she didn't think existed anymore. They were letters that Walter Lippmann had written to her in 1937 when they were carrying on their affair, unbeknownst to her husband. And it was because of these letters, which fell accidentally into Armstrong's hands, that he learned of the affair between his wife and his best friend—a discovery that ultimately led to their double divorces. She was so moved by this gift of Lippmann's lost love letters, it brought back such a flood of memories, that she wanted to talk to me about it. She had confidence in me and felt it was important that people understand this very emotional side of Lippmann's personality and his life. She said, "I know you've heard the various stories about our affair and the subsequent divorce and remarriage, but you've never heard the right story because only Walter and I know it." So she sat down and over the next few hours she told me this extraordinary story.

At the end she said, "I want you to come back, because not only do I have these four letters; I've also come across letters that Walter wrote me during this period which I didn't know still existed. When I assumed power of attorney, I went to the bank, and in the safe deposit box, underneath a sheaf of bonds, I discovered all the letters that Walter had written me during the time we were carrying on our affair. There were about sixty of them. They're so moving. I want you to read them and use them any way you see fit. But I don't have them here—I have to go to the bank to get them."

So we set a date when she would get the letters and bring them back to the apartment and show them to me. I had to make a trip to Europe, and it was about a month later when I came back. I called Helen, and we set a date when I would come by and read the letters. But just before our scheduled meeting she died very suddenly. This was a great shock, because nobody had expected it. She was a very high-strung person. I think she was consumed by anxiety and guilt and the combination was more than she could deal with.

Well, it turned out that the letters were not in her estate. In fact, they were nowhere to be found. I asked the executor of the estate if he had come across the letters. No. I asked her daughter, who was the inheritor of the estate. No. I asked everywhere. There was simply no trace of the letters. At that point I had given up. I thought, "I'll just have to go by what she told me." Then about six months later Louis Auchincloss called me and said, "Guess what? I've found the letters. They turned up in a safe deposit box I didn't even know about at the Bowery Savings Bank!"

I want to read you one letter to give you a sense of Lippmann's relationship with his wife. As I say, people were critical of her. But I think that in many ways she saved his life. She was a very vital, enthusiastic, temperamental Irish lady. Before he met her he had fallen into a stoical detachment that may have been very heroic but that didn't make him happy. I got a sense of how much she meant to him when I came across a letter he wrote her on her seventieth birthday, in 1967, at which point they had been married almost twenty years.

He wrote (for he was too shy to say it directly):

My dear Helen,

I feel I must write you a letter on this day. For in it I can say how happy I am that I married you and how deeply and everlastingly grateful I am. Looking back, I feel as if I had never really begun to live until we set out together, and that I have known from you not only unimagined happiness, but also the secret of starting life anew. You have been the decisive influence. But for you I would have settled down dully 30 years ago in the grooves I cut when I was young. But for you I would now be settling into a dull old age instead of feeling that we are at a new and fascinating beginning.

Helen died in February 1974. Lippmann's own life after that was very short—he died in December, at the age of eighty-five. But in the meantime his life took a final turn that was surprising to me. It was as if a terrible burden had been lifted. I think Helen's inability to deal with him made him feel very sad, and it was a relief not to have to deal with her anxiety about him. He became almost rejuvenated in a strange way. In the fall of that year he went up to Yale for the first time since he had given the university his papers ten years earlier. He went to look at the Walter Lippmann Room at the library and to reminisce over all the people who had been such an important part of life: William James and Santayana and Lincoln Steffens and Woodrow Wilson and Mabel Dodge and John Reed. He was very touched by that visit.

His host during the visit was Robert O. Anthony, a man to whom I am enormously indebted, as was Lippmann. A former telephone company executive, Anthony in the early 1930s, as a student, had begun collecting almost everything that Lippmann had ever written. In the 1960s, when Lippmann gave his papers to Yale, Anthony gave his own collection of Lippmann's published material to the university. It was he who achieved the enormous task of classifying not only Lippmann's published material, but his voluminous correspondence as well. Without Anthony's labor of love, and his generous cooperation, my own work would have been immensely more difficult, if not impossible.

That same fall Lippmann also received the Bronze Medallion from the city of New York. And he did something that was really quite remarkable, for him. The award was presented at Gracie Mansion by Mayor Abe Beame, who was of course New York's first Jewish mayor. Lippmann said to Mayor Beame, "I was born only a few blocks from here, but my ancestors, like yours, were immigrants." I think that's something he couldn't have said some years earlier. He seemed to be engaged in an effort to reassemble his past and to come to terms with it.

For me, Lippmann became not just an intellectual subject, but somebody whose life I became very involved in as part of the effort to understand it. I came to respect Lippmann enormously, even though I didn't always agree with or even admire everything he did. I learned a great deal from a man who was not perfect, but who set the highest standards for himself. He was a man who understood, as he once wrote, that "if the moralist is to deserve a hearing among his fellows he must set himself this task, which is so much humbler than to command and so much more difficult than to exhort. He must seek to anticipate and to supplement the insight of his fellow men into the problems of their adjustment to reality." Walter Lippmann made that adjustment to reality his life's work. And whenever, during the long time I spent on this book, my own energies flagged, I tried to remember the very high standard that he had set for himself.

Q. Why did Lippmann give his papers to Yale?
A. The answer is a good moral for all of us: Yale asked for them. He was a graduate of Harvard, a member of the Harvard Board of Overseers, and I think he always assumed that Harvard would want his papers. Harvard, in its usual way, assumed that it would get his papers. But it never formally approached him. His friend Wilmarth Lewis, the Walpole scholar at Yale, urged him to leave his papers to Yale. He persuaded Lippmann that this would be the right place because Colonel House's papers were at Yale, and the Charles Lindbergh papers, and the Henry Stimson papers, and they would dovetail nicely into his collection. Also,

Yale was going to create a Walter Lippmann Room, which indeed it did, with his memorabilia and his baseball cap and all that sort of thing.

At the end, of course, he left his money to Harvard, so his alma mater didn't come off so badly.

Q. Why did he switch from La Follette to Davis in the election of 1924?

A. He never supported La Follette. Also, at that time he was becoming increasingly conservative. I asked him why he voted for Landon in 1936 instead of FDR, which is an equivalent question, and he said, "Oh, I was just so conservative at that point." He had rejected so much of the whole Woodrow Wilson inheritance. During the twenties and the thirties he was an extremely conservative person; in fact, he was really quite conservative until the 1960s. So it was interesting to me that 1924 was the moment when he made this formal break with the Progressives. But as I went back and researched it, it seemed that it had been building up for some time.

Q. How could a moralist run off with his best friend's wife?

A. Well, I guess there are different kinds of morality. I don't know how to answer that question, but, for what it's worth, I thought it took more moral courage to do this than not to do it. He paid very dearly for his decision. He was ostracized by much of the social world that he cared about. It was a public scandal. He was taking an enormous risk. Here's a man who was forty-eight years old, who was the most eminent political commentator of his day, who was doing something scandalous, and he didn't know what effect it would have on his reputation. Indeed, he assumed that he would have to abandon his column—that the readers wouldn't stand for it. He was prepared to go into academia or even retire to Europe and write books. I think that was a courageous decision. He didn't know it would work out as well as it did, but he paid a social price for it nonetheless.

Q. At the beginning of your talk you spoke about the judgmental nature of the biographer. I keep thinking about Sergeant Friday's stricture, "Just the facts, ma'am." Is it necessary that a biographer be so judgmental?

A. Well, maybe it's not necessary, but I think one has to try to make some sense out of the material. It's a delicate path to walk. I tried not to be any more judgmental than seemed absolutely necessary, but there were times when I felt that I simply had to pull the material together—and also give some indication of what I thought about it, without being too heavy-handed. But I don't really believe in facts—I mean, I don't believe that facts exist in any significant way. I think that reality is not about facts, but about the relationship of facts to one another. In what I consider Lippmann's greatest book, *Public Opinion,* he says that people have no trouble accepting the fact that there are many opinions, but they can't accept that there are many sides to a "fact." And facts are often determined by how you see an issue, by the predisposition that you bring to it. I felt that in certain cases I just had to pull together the material in a way that expressed a point of view. Otherwise it would have been an encyclopedia entry.

Q. At what age did you become interested in Lippmann?

A. I was thirty-six. Actually I didn't meet him first at the Century Club. I'll tell you a little story, which is more interesting. I had been living in Europe during the sixties as a free-lance journalist, and I came back to Washington on an excursion ticket for a few days. I had been reading Lippmann's columns in the Paris *Herald Tribune,* and I thought—you know how it is when you're in a place for a short time, you do things you wouldn't dream of doing if you lived there—"I'm only going to be here for three days and I'd like to meet him." So I looked up his name in the phone book and there it was: Walter Lippmann, Woodley Road. I rang up the number and got his secretary, and I said who I was and what I had written, and that I'd like to meet Mr. Lippmann. She said, "Well, I don't know. I'll ask him and I'll try to call you back." About half an hour later I got a call. It was a sort of wispy voice, and it was Lippmann, and he said, "I've read some of your things. Could you come and have tea with me this afternoon?"

So I went to his house, this dark Tudor mansion on

Woodley Road. Helen opened the door, and we went into the study, and I spent about forty-five minutes there, talking with him about the state of the world and our mutual admiration for General de Gaulle. Later on I thought that was a remarkable thing for him to do. But he was somebody who liked to meet younger journalists. Since he didn't work at a newspaper office it was his way of being in touch. He'd never tell you what he thought. He always wanted to know what everybody else thought. He was a sponge. He wanted to get information. And then he filtered it through that wonderful analytical mind.

JEAN STROUSE

The Real Reasons

About one hundred years ago an eminent Victorian said: "There are two reasons why a man does anything. There's a good reason, and there's the real reason." The author of that remark wasn't Sigmund Freud or William James. Nor was it Henry James or Anthony Trollope. It was J. Pierpont Morgan. Not noted for his psychological insights or literary gifts, Morgan was nonetheless a shrewd judge of character—and his line about the real reasons could stand as a sort of credo for modern biography.

In trying to see some of the reasons why people do the things they do, modern biography operates at the intersections of public and private experience. It examines the ways in which character affects and is affected by social circumstance. And it asks how, in very specific contexts, particular people go through the processes of their lives. Biography also tells, of course, a good deal about the past; in the middle of the nineteenth century Emerson announced, "There is properly no history, only biography." But life studies don't tell only about the past; our approaches to history reflect the ideas and concerns of the present. You could, in fact, say that every age gets the biographies it deserves—that the assumptions we make and the questions we ask about other people's lives serve as tacit guides to our own.

The best biographies have always told wonderful stories. The subject almost doesn't matter if the writer brings enough magic to the task—though it's not magic, of course, that keeps you turning pages as if you were reading a great novel. Good biographers combine the arts of the novelist, the detective work of the historian and the insights of the psychologist.

Take, for example, a literary biography of P. G. Wodehouse by the British music critic Benny Green. The book is so specifically about the work and not the life that it deals with Wodehouse's early childhood in three pages and his marriage in one sentence. Still, it's quite sharp and very funny in its large biographical insights and specific probes. Green begins his last chapter with a disquisition on Victorian parenthood:

The Aunt, the Nanny and the Governess, that unholy trinity of shuffled-off responsibilities, so dominate the nineteenth-century landscape that the social historian, rummaging for an epithet of definition, can only mourn the absence from the language of a feminine equivalent to 'avuncular.' The callousness in this regard of the Victorian British middle classes, whose sense of imperial mission persuaded parents to suffer the little children to come unto somebody else, remains one of the wonders of the civilized world.

Wodehouse himself was dumped at about the age of three with a succession of hired women and aunts in England while his parents carried on the work of empire in Hong Kong. He claimed in all formal accounts to have had an idyllic childhood. Yet late in life he told a biographer that he and his brothers felt "almost like orphans," and that they "looked upon mother more like an aunt." Benny Green then quotes Wodehouse's fictional Bertie Wooster on the subject of his Aunt Agatha:

Aunt Agatha was one of those strong-minded women. She has an eye like a man-eating fish. . . . My experience is that when Aunt Agatha wants you to do a thing you do it, or else you find yourself wondering why those fellows in the olden days made such a fuss when they had trouble with the Spanish Inquisition.

Green goes on:

Wodehouse's world is littered with the bleached bones of aunts who failed to measure up to the modest requirements of common decency. Wooster is actually convinced that they are the cause of all the trouble in the world, remarking that "it has probably occurred to all thinking men that something drastic ought to be done about aunts," even stating his willingness to enroll in any society dedicated to their suppression. He tells Jeeves that "behind every poor, innocent, harmless blighter who is going down for the third time in the soup, you will find, if you look carefully enough, the aunt who shoved him into it."

Now Benny Green has just skillfully traversed here from a large point about Victorian Britain—a point that connects imperialism, sex roles, child-rearing practices, class distinctions, and social hypocrisy—to a witty set of textual examples that give fictional life to those abstractions and also move laughingly beyond them.

A very different sort of book, about a very different sort of man, is Edmund Morris's excellent biography of Theodore Roosevelt. (By the way, in discussing the Morris biography I don't mean in any way to slight David McCullough, who also wrote a first-rate book about Teddy Roosevelt. In fact, the coexistence of these two biographies illustrates an important point, which is that there is not just one true story about any of these lives; there are instead *versions* of the past, interpretive readings that give narrative coherence to history and character but don't claim the status of gospel. So here you had, in the case of Teddy Roosevelt, two top-flight biographers at work on the same material, and they came up with quite different stories, both excellent.)

Edmund Morris describes young Teddy Roosevelt, who was called "Teedie" by his family, as a gawky boy with a passion for natural history. Morris writes:

As Teedie turned fourteen, he blossomed into a grotesque flower of adolescence, offensive alike to eye, ear and nostril. Mittie Roosevelt [his mother], fresh and crackling in her perpetual white silks and muslin, must have suppressed many a shudder as she contemplated him. Apart from the owlish spectacles and snarling teeth, there was the overlong hair, its childish yellow darkening now to dirty blond; the bony wrists and ankles, which protruded every day a little farther from his carefully tailored suit; the fingers stained with ink and chemicals; the clumsy movements and too-quick reflexes. . . . Most of the time he reeked gently of arsenic: on days when he had been disemboweling as well as skinning his specimens, it was best to stand upwind of him.

When the Roosevelt family traveled to Europe in 1872, the parents parked Teedie and his brother Elliott with a German family called Minkwitz in Dresden for the summer so that the boys could become fluent in German. The future President of the United States did not at first make an agreeable impression on his hosts. They confiscated his arsenic and threw his dead mice out the window. "Undeterred," writes Morris, TR "continued to flay, pickle and stuff a variety of local fauna." He decorated the outside of the house with drying animal skins, and one night, "during a thunderstorm so violent the Minkwitzes hid between their mattresses, Teedie was heard to murmur in his sleep, 'Oh, it is raining and my hedgehog will be all spoiled.'"

Morris here shows TR from the outside as the gawky adolescent who gives his white-silk-clad mother the shudders—the odd duck (kids today might call him a nerd) obsessed with his smelly specimens—while at the same time creating enormous sympathy for the young, rather endearing eccentric ardently pursuing whatever interests him, from pickled mice to girls to political power.

These entertaining passages show Green and Morris working at the single most important element in biography—the delineation of character. To swipe Vince Lombardi's famous line about winning at sports, in biography character isn't everything—it's the only thing. Rendering that essential thing in prose, however, is about as simple as winning the World Series. Edmund Morris has said that he thinks a biographer ought to be "transparent," by which I assume he means that the biographer ought to shape and control the narrative unobtrusively, more or less the way the great nineteenth-century novelists did. In the selections I've just quoted, Morris invites readers physically into the scene through vivid sensual details, documenting what was actually going on and moving from the facts to an imaginative reading of character. He shows how he works, and an attentive reader can decide whether or not to trust this "transparent" narrative.

Benny Green, writing about Wodehouse, takes a different but equally useful tack. He simply doesn't accept Wodehouse's account of his idyllic childhood as the whole story; he brings in other "evidence" as well —the evidence of the novelist's literary work, for instance, and its persistent theme of domineering women. Green never says anything clunky or psychoanalytic about Wodehouse's mother, yet he shows that there was a large gap between the writer's autobiographical claim to childhood bliss and the comically rendered terrors consistently depicted in his fiction.

In the late twentieth century it seems obvious that one ought not to take anybody's autobiographical version of things at face value. To put it in Pierpont Morgan's terms, most people choose to see only the "good reasons" in their own lives, and the task of finding the "real reasons" is usually left to biographers, historians, psychologists, and occasionally husbands, wives, and friends. But this kind of skepticism is relatively new. And it has had a profound effect on the craft of biography. The big biographies of the nineteenth century were essentially chronicles, focused primarily on public experience. They provided exhaustive—and sometimes exhausting—accounts of what *happened* in the daily lives of great men, in order to illuminate the large arenas of war, politics, religion, literature, and art in which such men performed. These monumental tributes were almost always respectful, if not reverential. They told about the "good reasons" and didn't fool around with questions of motivation or conflict. They took people's word for it, whatever "it" might be, and did not venture into interpretive waters. Most of these writers simply ignored disturbing facts that didn't fit in with their notions of decorum.

The biographer's job, then, was to tell the story of a life that was somehow exemplary—which suggests that nineteenth-century readers were looking for models, guides to the moral and material universe. Mothers would read books about the mothers of George Washington and Thomas Jefferson to see how you'd go about raising a little boy to be a great man. Pierpont Morgan's mother gave him a biography of George Washington for Christmas in 1845, when the boy was eight years old. Washington, of course, provided a model of American leadership—self-abnegating, democratic, absolutely uninterested in power for its own sake. Morgan admired Washington for the rest of his life and eventually bought many of the first President's letters for his famous manuscript collection. But he was even more interested in Napoleon, who wielded a very different kind of power and whose imperial ambitions and complex character were arguably more intriguing than Washington's—certainly to this particular adolescent boy they were.

Right there is an illustration of one of the differences between nineteenth- and twentieth-century approaches to biography. Of course a nineteenth-century mother would encourage her son to see himself as a future George Washington; of course a mid-century boy would find Napoleon's career fascinating. But in the 1980s nothing in this line is taken as a matter of course. What does the gift of a Washington biography say about Mrs. Morgan's expectations of her eldest son? Why Washington instead of Jefferson, or Tom Paine? What are the moral lessons of this particular book? What other reading material did she and her husband give their son? How else did they communicate their ambitions and hopes? And what was it that fascinated young Morgan about Napoleon? How did he imagine his future? What battles did he want to wage and what kind of power did he want to wield?

Of course there aren't simple or literal answers to those questions, but whatever can be learned about them will illuminate the complex process that made

Pierpont Morgan who he was, and help in the search for the "real reasons" of his life.

Lytton Strachey, in his preface to *Eminent Victorians* (1918), marked the turn toward a more interpretive approach and virtually prescribed a methodology for modern biography when he complained that the history of the Victorian age would never be written because "we know too much about it." The first requisite of the historian, he announced, is

. . . ignorance, which simplifies and clarifies, which selects and omits, with a placid perfection unattainable by the highest art. . . . It is not by the direct method of a scrupulous narration that the explorer of the past can hope to depict that singular epoch. If he is wise, he will adopt a subtler strategy. He will attack his subject in unexpected places; he will fall upon the flank, or the rear; he will shoot a sudden, revealing searchlight into obscure recesses, hitherto undivined. He will row out over that great ocean of material, and lower down into it, here and there, a little bucket, which will bring up to the light of day some characteristic specimen, from those far depths, to be examined with a careful curiosity.

In quoting this passage of Strachey's and discussing Pierpont Morgan's notion of real reasons, I don't want to sound like an advocate of psychobiography. Strachey was talking about art—the art of selection, omission, and suggestive incident—and it is just that quality of artfulness that is lacking in much of the twentieth century's eager application of psychology to history, literature and biography. Instead of subtly exploring the past with a "revealing searchlight," too many modern writers have tried to go at it with a kind of intellectual can opener. The jargon and smug reductionism of this work fail to give any sense of the richness or complexity of the past. In fact, they might be said to constitute a serious crime against human nature.

The task of writing a biography of Alice James brought up for me with special urgency the question of biographical interpretation. There was no exciting plot line to Alice's life. She was an obscure neurasthenic, with a couple of famous brothers, who spent a good deal of time confined to a sickbed. All the drama of her life took place in private, rather like the stories in her brother Henry's novels. By contrast, Pierpont Morgan's large public life connected at every turn with major events in America's history and assumed mythic proportions in the American imagination. It's not an accident that I've chosen two such opposite kinds of stories: after spending five interesting years thinking and writing about a powerless female invalid in a family of intellectuals, I wanted a complete change—and ended up with the most powerful man of the late nineteenth century. Morgan's story leads along very different paths—into the worlds of international finance, politics, art and rare-book collecting, and across the

Atlantic to England, France, Italy and Egypt—and it presents very different kinds of biographical questions. I'm not yet ready to talk about those questions—I probably won't be for about four years—but I can tell you about the Jameses, who lend themselves quite specifically to the discussion of biographical method.

I hadn't thought much about the difference between "good" and "real" reasons until I had finished a first draft of Alice James's life that just didn't work. Partly it didn't work because what the Jameses had to say about themselves and each other was so opaque, elusive and confusing that it practically needed a translator. And partly it didn't work because much of what was going on among all the people in that family wasn't visible to the naked eye.

For example, the grown James siblings described their childhood as pure paradise. Alice, looking back, in a diary she began when she was almost forty, wrote: "It seems now incredible to me that I should have drunk, as a matter of course, at that ever springing fountain of responsive love and bathed all unconscious in that flood of human tenderness." She described her mother's "extraordinary selfless devotion, as if she simply embodied the unconscious essence of wife and motherhood." And Alice's brother Henry echoed these sentiments, in effect nominating their mother for sainthood:

[174

She was patience. She was wisdom. She was exquisite maternity . . . one can feel, forever, the inextinguishable vibration of her devotion. . . . It was a perfect mother's life—the life of a perfect wife. To bring her children into the world—to expend herself, for years, for their happiness and welfare— then, when they had reached a full maturity and were absorbed in the world and in their own interests—to lay herself down in her ebbing strength and yield up her pure soul to the celestial power that had given her this divine commission.

Sounds like everybody we know, right?

There's a good deal of evidence to suggest that Mary James bore no resemblance to this portrait of divine maternity. All five of her children suffered most of their lives with crippling emotional troubles. Depression, nervous breakdown, alcoholism, homosexuality, and various psychosomatic ailments were on the collective list. Perhaps, as the Jameses liked to think, genetics had something to do with all these difficulties, but it's hard now to see such polymorphous suffering as unrelated to the unique experience of this particular family. Mary James seems to have been a cold, practical, supervisory mother, who had little sympathy for any sign of weakness and no patience with the frequent illnesses that plagued her children.

The uncomplaining Henry was her favorite, her "angel." But even he wasn't safe from her intrusions.

When he was traveling abroad in the 1870s she wrote anxious, hovering questions: was he eating well, sleeping enough, spending too much money? She missed him and longed, she wrote, "to fold you in my own tenderest embrace—It seems to me darling Harry that your life must need this succulent, fattening element more than you know yourself."

Her darling Harry was over thirty by this time and quite liked being across the Atlantic, three thousand miles away from his beloved family and its high-calorie emotional diet. Mary James had another little suggestion to make. "I know of only one thing that would solve the difficulty and harmonize the discordant elements in your life," she wrote. "You would make dear Harry according to my estimate, the most loving and loveable and happiest of husbands. I wish I could see you in a favorable attitude of heart toward the divine institution of marriage." Henry quietly ignored her, answering lightly, "If you will provide the wife, the fortune and the 'inclination,' I will take them all."

She could not, needless to say, provide the inclination, although she may well have been tempted to arrange for the wife and the fortune. In fact, the complicated folds of her own "tenderest embrace" may have had a good deal to do with her favorite son's lifelong disinclination in this direction. As Leon Edel has pointed out, the mothers in Henry James's novels are grasping, selfish, demanding, often terrifying creatures. At least two of them resemble vultures or vampires, feeding off the spirits of their innocent children. Others are so remote and self-absorbed as to be irrelevant except as obstructions. Even the obtuse, hapless, hypochondriacal mother in *Daisy Miller* exerts a negative influence on her daughter's fate through her signal failure to notice what is really happening to Daisy. That Henry James never created in fiction a mother imbued with anything like the divine selflessness he attributed to Mary James suggests that he recognized aspects of her character that were more complex than perfection.

The "evidence," then, for the story of the James family childhood lies not in the noble sentiments expressed by all the children once they grew up. Those eloquent tributes to divine maternity and ever-springing fountains of responsive love express the "good reasons" for the distinctive shaping of their characters. The evidence for the real reasons lies elsewhere—in the parents' observable behavior and in the indirect testimony of illness, fiction, personal interactions, moral preoccupations, and the themes of Henry's and William's adult works. And the truth about their childhood experience probably rests somewhere in between this garden-of-Eden myth and some fairly prickly realities. For the myth shouldn't be discounted as mere propaganda: it serves as an important guide to what the Jameses wanted or were supposed to believe about their lives, and that in itself tells a great deal about them. Their collective desire to canonize the past and their parents had to do not only with a common human impulse to see childhood as idyllic, but also with specific pressures and notions that dominated their extraordinary early lives.

Their father, Henry James, Sr., devoted his life to the theological repudiation of *his* father's angry Calvinist God—and to giving his own children as free, sensuous and liberal an upbringing as he'd felt his own to have been constricted, austere and cold. As a writer and thinker-about-town he could be delightfully irreverent. He once described the high-minded Boston Brahmins as "simmering in their own fat and putting a nice brown on each other." He had been introduced by Emerson to Thomas Carlyle in London in the early 1840s and had taken an instant dislike to the sage of Chelsea. Years later, just after Carlyle's death, James wrote in the *Atlantic Monthly:* "Thomas Carlyle is incontestably dead at last, by the acknowledgment of all newspapers. I had, however, the pleasure of an intimate intercourse with him when he was an infinitely deader man than he is now."

James eventually formulated a religion of his own, loosely based on Swedenborgianism, though his writings on the subject were so murky that when he published a book called *The Secret of Swedenborg,* William Dean Howells objected that James had "kept it." One measure of his success at becoming a more permissive, less terrifying parent than his own father had been is the fact that when he published a book called *Substance and Shadow; Or Morality and Religion in Their Relation to Life: An Essay on the Physics of Creation,* his son William, then twenty, designed for the title page a woodcut of a man beating a dead horse.

Henry, Sr., was a genial but confusing and highly contradictory man, who adored his brilliant oldest sons, William and Henry, Jr., but did not equate writing novels or a distinguished career in psychology and philosophy with success. He had urged on all five of his children a strenuous individualism that stressed *being extraordinary,* no matter what one actually chose to do. When William wanted to become a painter his father urged him toward science, and when he became a scientist his father complained that the scientific world was too narrowing. In fact, choosing to be anything at all in this unusual scheme led to paternal disappointment, for in turning toward one field you were inevitably turning away from other possibilities.

From very early on, William, Henry and Alice learned to convert the raw data of their own ideas and feelings into interesting forms of communication, for perception and articulate expression were the principal ingredients of a Jamesian success. These preoccupations fostered in three of the young Jameses a fine-tuned self-awareness. But inevitably there were great holes in what they could see about the experiences that shaped their lives. Because they were expected simultaneously to reinforce the myth of family divinity and to present private perceptions of truth for public consumption, the James children grew adept at giving eloquently ambiguous voice to the way things were supposed to be. They learned to see and not see, say and not say, reveal and conceal, all at the same time. In their struggles to find some resolution that would accommodate both "good" and "real" reasons, William, Henry and Alice James became intellectual explorers who conducted guided tours through the far reaches of the human mind.

William examined his own experience with insatiable curiosity throughout his life—swallowing drugs as if he lived in the 1960s, attending the sessions of spiritualists, mediums and "psychics," trying to peer into the wellsprings of his elations and depressions and understand the complex interactions between mind and body. His sister Alice, in her diary, summed up his mercurial temperament and passionate curiosity after she'd asked him to describe a country house he had bought in Chocorua, New Hampshire, in 1886. William "expressed himself and his environment to perfection," she noted, when he replied, "Oh, it's the most delightful house you ever saw; has 14 doors all opening outside." Alice observed wryly, "His brain isn't limited to 14, perhaps unfortunately."

William James invented the phrase "stream of consciousness" and once, in a letter to his wife, wrote a definition of character that belongs on every biographer's bulletin board next to J. P. Morgan's quote about real reasons: "I've often thought that the best way to define a man's character would be to seek out the particular mental or moral attitude in which, when it came upon him, he felt himself most deeply and intensely active and alive. At such moments there is a voice inside which speaks and says, 'This is the real me!'" It took William James a long time to find that sense of his own integrity, and in the process he articulated the principles of pragmatism in philosophy, turned his powerful mental searchlight on the varieties of religious experience, and pushed back the boundaries of nineteenth-century psychology.

His sister Alice, who spent most of her life suffering from mysterious ailments that were variously diagnosed as hysteria, neurasthenia, spinal neurosis, and nervous hyperesthesia, very much approved William's mapping of this psychological territory when she read his *Principles of Psychology* in 1890. A year later, as she was dying of cancer, she wrote to him: "When I am gone, pray don't think of me simply as a creature who might have been something else, had neurotic science been born." She used "neurotic" in its nineteenth-century sense, referring to nervous disorders, but it amounts to about the same thing we mean by the word.

Her poignant plea acknowledged that her life had been a failure. But in stoically saying, "Don't make excuses for me, take me for what I am, limitations and all," she shows the strength of character that did give her a measure of philosophical integrity. In the last few years of her life she began to keep a diary and to find a voice of her own in that family of strong, articulate voices. The journal doesn't triumph resoundingly over adversity; it doesn't burst with hidden genius. Its subject is human suffering, and its achievement is the working out of an attitude that accepts and moves beyond personal pain. In some ways, this attitude resembles Christian patience, but Alice clung too fiercely to the unique quality of her own experience and was too much the daughter of her iconoclastic Swedenborgian father to find solace in conventional faith.

She moved in the late 1880s toward an untutored existentialism that regarded only the present and made experience its religion. When her cancer was diagnosed, she wrote to William that the approach to death was "the most supremely interesting moment in life . . . It is as simple in one's own person as any fact of nature, the fall of a leaf or the blooming of a rose, and I have a delicious consciousness, ever present, of wide spaces close at hand and whisperings of release in the air."

Where their father had been obsessed with the workings of a divine order, three of the James children concentrated on the baffling intricacies of human character. They did not ignore God—William worried and wrote about Him, Alice somewhat ironically assumed His providence, and Henry's novels have strong Christian undertones. But the younger generation of Jameses turned from the scrutiny of God to the scrutiny of man, and Henry in particular wrote about the varieties of human experience with such range and depth that fiction has not been the same since.

"To live over people's lives is nothing," he once said, "unless we live over their perceptions, live over the growth, the change, the varying intensity of the same —since it was *by* these things they themselves lived." His novels are about the growth, change and varying intensity of perceptions. What happens doesn't matter nearly as much as what people *see* about what happens, and the moral universe turns on the consequences not of action but of perception. His great theme was the confrontation of two worlds, American and European —one innocent, fresh, unabashed, energetic and relatively simple; the other rich, dense, knowing, intricately subtle and complex. The protagonists of the novels, usually women, start out in relative innocence and slowly come to see a range and depth of experience larger than anything they could previously have imagined.

It was this process of learning to see that fascinated Henry James. And it was the ability to open out one's imaginative vision to take in all the human dichotomies of good and evil, innocence and knowledge, myth and reality, new world and old, that, for him, constituted living in the largest sense. Freud once said that man's self-esteem had received three great blows from post-Renaissance science: a cosmological blow, when Copernicus proved that the earth was not the center of the universe; a biological blow, when Darwin showed that man was not organically superior to animals; and a psychological blow, when psychoanalysis asserted that "the ego is not master in its own house." Before these dramatic intellectual revolutions, the *whys* of human behavior—the effort to see into the real reasons at work beneath the surface of everyday life—were left to poets, prophets, preachers and novelists. Since Darwin and Freud advanced their ideas, however—we might add Picasso, Marx and Einstein to the list—questions of motivation and of the powerful dynamics at work inside and beyond apparently ordinary events have raised their querulous heads in all fields of intellectual, scientific and cultural life.

I said before that every age gets the biographies it deserves—that the questions we ask about the past reflect our present ideas and concerns. But maybe I should have said every age gets the stories it *needs*. Future historians may characterize the late twentieth century by its sense of fragmentation, its lack of confidence in history's progress, its loss of consensus about what an "exemplary" life might be. People still long for models of wholeness, though—for evidence that individual lives and choices matter. Modern biography tells not *how to live,* but how other people, in all their interesting, quirky, original variety, have lived. It shows a saintly mystic who treated his family abominably, for instance, or an ordinary housewife whose character had in it strains of heroism, or a famous love story that was no less confused and ambiguous than the neighbors' marriage, or a great statesman who did measure up in private to the dignity and integrity of his public reputation. Maybe, in fact, biography is uniquely equipped just now to look at the fragments and chaos of the past through methods of modern inquiry—careful research into primary sources, fresh angles of approach, skepticism, special kinds of "listening" for new evidence—and to shape out of those materials a narrative whole with a human life at its center.

Q. Are there many descendants of the James family still in the Boston area?

A. Not many. There's an amusing story about one of them, though—a great-grandson of William's, I think, who grew up in Cambridge, Massachusetts, and got thoroughly sick of everybody saying every time he was introduced, "Oh, James—any relation to Henry and William?" He went out to Colorado, where people said, "Oh, James—any relation to Frank and Jesse?" He stayed in Colorado.

Q. What was Henry James's obscure hurt, which is never explained?

A. It seems to have been some sort of injury that he received in his late teens or early twenties. It's not clear exactly what it was. He writes about it in his autobiography in suggestive, mysterious imagery, making it sound like some kind of sexual wound. Leon Edel explored this question thoroughly in his outstanding life of Henry James—Edel looked through doctors' records, family and friends' diaries and letters, and old newspaper accounts, thinking that if there had been a major traumatic injury it would have been mentioned. It wasn't. Edel thinks that Henry probably injured his back, and speculates that the novelist described it as personal and private and "intimate" at least in part because he didn't fight in the Civil War, which started just about the same time; in fact, James blurs the dates a little in his autobiography, making the injury occur earlier than it actually did, perhaps to provide an excuse for not having served in the Union army. Fighting was of course the appropriate, patriotic, masculine thing to do—and an "obscure hurt" might make a useful justification for taking another path. Still, it's a cloudy question. James did suffer with serious back trouble for the rest of his life, so I'm inclined to agree with Edel's diagnosis.

Q. How did William James characterize his mother?

A. He called her "healthy-minded," which was not a compliment. She was in fact very tough on him. He was something of a hypochondriac. Unlike Henry, who was very stiff-upper-lip about all his problems and went away across the Atlantic and didn't talk about them, William was a complainer. He fell apart quite regularly, and his mother had no patience with his difficulties. I think he meant indirectly that "healthy-minded" people are the kind who constantly tell you to pull up your socks and get on with it, and they don't understand the kinds of troubles he and his siblings had to deal with. William married a woman who was healthy-minded in a better sense—she wasn't at all sickly, and she managed to cope with real life, children, houses, moving, et cetera, and to allow William to go off and do his work. Actually it was quite a good marriage. So he found a better version of that healthy-mindedness—and it helped him quite a lot.

Q. What led you to Alice James?

A. Partly it was an accident. I was working as an editor in a publishing house, and I wanted to leave that and do some writing, and I thought biography would be a reasonable form to work in because I like telling stories but not having to make the whole thing up. One summer I was reading a book by Calvin Tomkins called *Living Well Is the Best Revenge*, which is about Gerald and Sara Murphy, and at one point the Mur-

phys come back from Paris to Cambridge, Massachusetts, and drop in on Alice James and her circle. I
thought, "Oh, well, if Alice James had a circle she must
have been interesting." I vaguely knew that Henry
James had had a sister, but I didn't know anything
about her. I began digging around and found her diary,
which was out of print but available in secondhand
stores, and a book by F. O. Mathiessen called *The James
Family*, which is really about William and Henry and
Alice and which takes her mind seriously, using her
diary and her letters. And just at that point I needed
someone of Mathiessen's stature to say, "Yes, this is an
interesting person; you're right to be curious about
her." Still, I hesitated because her life was so depressing
and limited—I was afraid I couldn't stand to be around
her for what I thought would take two years. (It turned
out to take five.)

But finally I decided there were enough things in her
life that fascinated me to offset the negatives. Here was
an extraordinary family of characters—two real geniuses, a couple of other, ne'er-do-well brothers, a father
who was something of a genius himself—and they
were all absorbed with one another and with their own
experiences, so they wrote all the time, and you had a
wonderful record of what was going on because they
were amazingly articulate. I wanted to know what it
was like to be not a famous person—and a girl—in this
family, how social history questions about femininity

in the late nineteenth century came into Alice's story, all about the nervous disorders that she was struggling with, and how science was thinking about those physical/psychological problems. All those things would keep me going, I thought, even when Alice got too depressing—and she sometimes did.

So I decided to go ahead, and I quit my job and got a small advance from a publisher and went to work. Then I went back to that book by Calvin Tomkins, and it turned out that the visit to Alice James and her circle didn't take place until 1923, by which time my Alice James had been dead for thirty years. It was a reference to William's wife, who was also named Alice. So I guess the moral is, if you're looking for something you find it, whether it's there or not.

Q. I'm just trying to understand the genesis of your book. You say that you wrote a first draft and that it somehow didn't hang together and didn't make sense, so you went back and tried to understand the mythology of the James family.

A. What I had done in that first draft was set up endless passages quoting the Jameses on their early lives and what had happened. And it was confusing and opaque—it didn't tell the full story. I then realized—very reluctantly—that I had to step in, in my own voice, and tell the family story, before their own words would make sense. In other words, I had to show what I considered to be the real dynamics of the situation.

For instance, when Alice talks about "ever-springing fountains of responsive love" and the "essence of divine maternity," I had to have already established the character of Mary James and the reasons why Alice was supposed to think that, so you could hear it in context. Otherwise a reader can't see through the "good" reasons to the real ones.

But I had been afraid of getting in there in my own voice. I had thought that I wouldn't have to talk much about Henry and William—I could just do Alice off on one side, and wouldn't impose myself on the narrative or do any interpreting. So getting brave enough to venture my own views was really what writing the book was all about. The first part was just sort of long notes.

Q. The danger, I imagine, is that once you set up the mythology and try to make it hang together, you force it to have a coherence that it didn't have.

A. Yes, I think that's a big danger. But it's also true that as you live through the processes of these lives you do begin to see some coherence, certain kinds of connections, and when you construct a narrative out of these raw materials, you're drawing the connections together. The best check on the problem of forcing a false coherence is to present the evidence as much as possible, to show how you're making your conclusions, so that a reader can go along with you and say, "That's right; that's not right." Because, after all, it's only one version of the story. I mean, you're not just taking numbers two, three and four and adding them up and getting a result that everybody could agree on. You're selecting certain evidence and you're drawing ideas from it, trying to make sense out of it. If you didn't, you'd just have undigested facts which wouldn't be interesting to read. But you're right—it's a dangerous tightrope to walk.

Q. Did you feel that Alice James really did have the potential of her two genius brothers but was just inhibited by being a woman? And the social circumstances?

A. I really don't. I don't think she was a genius. She was very smart and she had a facility with language, and if she hadn't been so stifled she might have been a good political journalist or historian of some kind, although women hardly ever did that kind of work in those days. I doubt that she had the real fireworks that her two oldest brothers had. But that's just my guess. I tried to take her at her word when she said, "Please don't think of me as a creature who might have been something else." I tried to resist making her something that she wasn't.

Q. Did you like *Alice James?*

A. Sometimes yes and sometimes no. My reactions to her were extremely complex and interesting, and at one point during the writing I got so mad at her that I just got completely stuck. Alice was in her late twenties and early thirties, and she was systematically closing down every option that might have led her away from a life of invalidism. She wasn't doing any intellectual work, although she had some that she could have been doing. She was being awful to every man who approached her and wasn't even very nice to her female friends. She was turning into a tyrannical invalid who collapsed in order to get people to take care of her. And I hated it. I really got so mad that I couldn't continue writing. It was amazing, because I had known all along that that's how the story was going to come out. That's why I had hesitated at the beginning—because the story seemed too depressing. But I had decided to go ahead, and thought I'd dealt with the problem—until, at this point in the process of writing, I just got too furious at her to go on. What I did was take a month off. And I remembered that Erik Erikson had had a similar problem when he was writing his biography of Gandhi. He had been writing about this saintly man and then he found out how awful Gandhi was to his family, and he was horrified. I think he actually sat down and wrote out all his objections in a letter to Gandhi—who wasn't around anymore to receive it, of course—but that was Erikson's way of working out the problem. In my case, I didn't write it out, but I had long conversations with Alice and Henry in my head.

What happens, I think, is that in writing about someone's whole life you get involved in it day by day, as it evolves, and other options besides the ones that the person ultimately chose do seem open. The life takes on a kind of fictional reality to you as you're reimagining it. So there you are writing, and Alice is twenty-five years old, and you think all sorts of things could happen, even though you know they didn't, and there's an energy to that. You get involved, even if you dislike the person or have trouble with him or her; you care about this story that you're spending so much time on. And I just didn't want it to have such a sad ending. So I put it aside for a while, and one thing I realized in the course of taking that "vacation" was that Alice also wanted her life to have turned out better. She was very competitive with her brothers. She was fiercely ambitious and intelligent, and the strength of her paralysis and incapacity was also the measure of her ambition. And so the conflict was very real in her, in those years, and I think I was picking that up, from her letters and diary. What I eventually came to was a fuller understanding of the conflict in her, based on my own intense reaction to it. I also came to see clearly that the interesting story was what *did* happen, not the way either she or I would have liked it to happen, and that who she was, rather than who she might have been, was the important thing. The unhappy ending was the real point of the story.

Q. That was about not *liking her. How about liking her?*

A. I'll tell you one more story, about an incident that

really surprised me; it shows how vivid biographical subjects can become to their authors. In 1976 I moved up to Cambridge, Massachusetts, to do my research, because most of the James family material is there, at Harvard's Houghton Library. One day I realized that the next day was Alice James's birthday, and I thought an interesting thing to do would be to visit her grave. It seemed like sort of a lark, almost a joke—what you're supposed to do when you're writing a biography. So I bought some daisies and got a little plastic cup and I went to the Cambridge Cemetery. The James plot is in the back, looking out over Soldier's Field Road—sort of a bleak highway—and nobody else was around. I got to the grave, and there were Henry and William, their parents, William's wife and his infant son, Hermann, and, of course, Alice. I put the daisies down on her grave and suddenly found myself in tears.

I was absolutely amazed, because I hadn't thought that there was much going on between Alice and me. And as soon as I started to cry I also had to laugh, because I realized that I was thinking: "Here are Henry and William, and everybody comes to see them, and probably nobody's been to visit Alice since her friend Katharine Loring got too old, fifty years ago," and I heard myself say, internally, to Alice: "Don't worry— I'll take care of you."

Well, there she was, after a hundred years, dead, and still getting somebody—in this case, me—to take care of her. That's what she did to everybody her whole life. And that experience taught me real lessons about the force and conflicts of her character. I tell it to you as an amusing story, but in fact all these emotional responses that you have as a biographer are important parts of the work. If you can hold yourself still and watch them, you'll learn an enormous amount about your subject. Because that's not just a story about me. It's also a story about Alice.

ROBERT A. CARO

Lyndon Johnson and the Roots of Power

Franklin D. Roosevelt first met Lyndon Johnson when Johnson, who was only twenty-eight years old, had just been elected to Congress. He had run on a platform that, he said, consisted of one word: "Roosevelt." During the entire campaign, that was his only theme: "Roosevelt. Roosevelt. One hundred percent for Roosevelt."

Lyndon Johnson had a great ability to charm older men who possessed the political power he wanted and who could help him get it. He was a master of flattery, you know. One of his techniques with these older men was literally to sit at their feet. If they were sitting in a chair, talking, he would sit on the floor, at their knee, with his face tilted up attentively, drinking in their words of wisdom. His flattery went to extremes in so many ways that his contemporaries called him a "professional son."

But Franklin Roosevelt's affection for Lyndon Johnson wasn't based merely on Johnson's flattery. In attempting to explain to me the basis for the President's rapport with the young congressman—a rapport almost unique in Roosevelt's life—one of Roosevelt's advisers, James H. Rowe, told me, "You have to understand that these were two great political geniuses. They could talk on the same level. Roosevelt had very few people he could talk to who could understand all the implications of what he was saying. But Lyndon, at the age of twenty-eight, could understand it all." Roosevelt, speaking of Johnson, once said to Harold Ickes, "You know, Harold, that's the kind of uninhibited young pro I might have been as a young man—if I hadn't gone to Harvard." Roosevelt also made a prediction. He said, "Harold, in the next couple of generations the balance of power in this country is going to shift to the South and the West. And that kid Lyndon Johnson could well be the first Southern President." Well, Roosevelt was right, as it turned out. And tonight I'm going to talk about Lyndon Johnson's race for that goal, his race along what I call "the path to power."

For me there were many obstacles in learning about that race, in learning about the young Lyndon Johnson and his early political career. Most of the obstacles were put there by Johnson himself. When he was President we saw what has been called an obsession with secrecy, and this obsession was striking, even when he was a young man—even when he was a college student, in fact. But perhaps the biggest obstacle was not him, but me—my background, which includes New York City, the Horace Mann school, Princeton, and an entire life spent in a city filled with museums and concerts, a life spent on crowded streets and sidewalks.

Lyndon Johnson was raised in the Hill Country of Texas. And that was about as different from my background—and, I suspect, from most of yours—as you can get. Often, during the seven years I was working on this book, I would be in New York one day, and the next day I would fly to Texas. In New York I might have been working in this very library with its marble halls and glittering chandeliers; I might have had lunch with other writers, and the talk might have been about abstractions or about literature. When I left the library that day I would walk out into crowds of people on the street. The next day I would fly to Austin and rent a car and drive west into the Hill Country. And it sometimes seemed to me on such a day that I was going from one end of the world to the other.

The Hill Country—its geologic name is the Edwards Plateau—covers twenty-four thousand square miles. That's an area so large you could drop several states into it and still have considerable space left over.

When Lyndon Johnson was growing up there its total population was about one person per square mile. Even today it's a vast and empty and lonely place, where you can drive long stretches without passing a single house or a car. The hills seem to go on forever—every time you get to the top of one ridge of hills there suddenly are more ridges in front of you. The first settlers called it the land of endless "false horizons."

I'll never forget my first view of Johnson City, the first time I realized how hard it was going to be for an urban person like me, the ultimate city boy, to understand Lyndon Johnson. I had driven out of Austin about forty-eight miles, and at the top of what I later learned was called Round Mountain—it's really just a tall hill, but it's the tallest hill around—I stopped the car. And in front of me this incredible empty panorama was stretching out literally as far as I could see. At first I thought there was nothing in it. And then all of a sudden, down below, off in the distance, I saw this tiny little huddle of houses, the place where Lyndon Johnson grew up. The Hill Country is a place where a predominant feature of life is loneliness. In fact, for a considerable portion of his boyhood, Johnson lived on a ranch off in the valley of the Pedernales River, a place even more isolated than Johnson City. His brother once talked to me about how he and Lyndon used to sit on a fence that bordered a road that ran alongside their ranch and wait for hours, hoping that just one single person would ride by so that they would have someone to talk to. The Hill Country was also a place of terrible poverty. One of Lyndon Johnson's best friends, to get some cash, once carried a dozen eggs to Marble Falls. To do that he had to ride all day, twenty-three miles across the hills, carrying the eggs in a box in front of him so that they wouldn't break. And the cash that he received for that day's trip was one dime.

The Hill Country is also a land where the people are honorable and honest, to a remarkable degree. I learned that if you could only find the right question to ask, you would always get an honest answer. The people are neighborly and helpful beyond belief, and they have their own quite wonderful wisdom. Still, the culture of the Hill Country was so different from the one in which I had been raised that one day I said to my wife, "I'm not really understanding these people, or Lyndon Johnson. We have to move to the Hill Country."

We moved to a house on the edge of the Hill Country, and for parts of three years I lived there with Ina, driving to lonely ranches and farms to interview the people who grew up and went to college with Lyndon Johnson and helped make up his first political machine.

There was a bright side to Lyndon Johnson's race to power, and a dark side. Let me talk about the bright side first.

The bright side is very bright. For Lyndon Johnson

was a genius at what his Hill Country populist fore-
bears would have defined as the highest art of government: the art of using the power of the sovereign state
to help its people, particularly the least fortunate
among them, people who couldn't help themselves,
who were fighting forces too big for them to fight
alone. His father, who was a passionately idealistic
rural legislator, had a wonderful phrase for it. He said
that the duty of government is to help people who are
"caught in the tentacles of circumstance."

When I was interviewing in the Hill Country, no
matter what I was talking to people about, I found that
one phrase was repeated over and over again: "He
brought the lights. No matter what Lyndon was like,
we loved him because he brought the lights." They
were talking about the fact that when Johnson became
congressman from the Hill Country in 1937, at the age
of twenty-eight, there was no electricity there. And by
1948, when he was elected to the Senate, most of the
district had electricity.

Because I was from New York City, and electricity
was always just *there*, the full significance of that fact
went right over my head for quite some time, I'm sorry
to say. I understood intellectually that he had brought
electricity, but I didn't understand what electricity
meant in the lives of impoverished farm families, or
what their lives had been like in this isolated and remote region without it. Because there was no electric-

ity, there were no movies. There were almost no radios; there were a few crystal sets, but the distances were too great—the Hill Country is so cut off from the rest of America that the people on its isolated farms couldn't get many programs. In fact, one of the most poignant things that was told to me was how they loved Roosevelt but never heard his wonderful voice. "We really loved Roosevelt here, and we always read about his wonderful 'fireside chats,' but we could never get to hear the 'fireside chats.' "

Because there was no electricity, there were no electric pumps, and water had to be hauled up—in most cases by the women on the farms and the ranches, because not only the men but the children, as soon as they were old enough to work, had to be out in the fields. The wells in the Hill Country were very deep because of the water table—in many places they had to be about seventy-five feet deep. And every bucket of water had to be hauled up from those deep wells. The Department of Agriculture tells us that the average farm family uses two hundred gallons of water a day. That's seventy-three thousand gallons, or three hundred tons, a year. And it all had to be lifted by these women, one bucket at a time.

I didn't know what this meant. And they had to show me. Those women would say to me, "You're a city boy. You don't know how heavy a bucket of water is, do you?" So they would get out their old buckets, and they'd go out to the no-longer-used wells and wrestle off the heavy covers that were always on them to keep out the rats and squirrels, and they'd lower a bucket and fill it with water. Then they'd say, "Now feel how heavy it is." And I would haul it up, and it *was* heavy. And they'd say, "It was too heavy for me. After a few buckets I couldn't lift the rest with my arms anymore." And they'd show me how they had lifted each bucket of water. They would lean into the rope and throw the whole weight of their bodies into it every time, leaning so far that they were almost horizontal to the ground. And then they'd say, "Do you know how I carried the water?" And they would bring out the yokes, which were like cattle yokes, so that they could carry one of the heavy buckets on each side.

And sometimes these women told me something that was so sad I never forgot it. I heard it many times, but I'll never forget the first woman who said it to me. She was a very old woman who lived on a very remote and isolated ranch—I had to drive hours just to get out there—up in the Hill Country near Burnet. She said, "Do you see how round-shouldered I am?" Well, indeed, I had noticed, without really seeing the significance, that many of these women, who were in their sixties or seventies, were much more stooped and bent than women, even elderly women, in New York. And she said: "I'm round-shouldered from hauling the water. I was round-shouldered like this well before my time, when I was still a young woman. My back got bent from hauling the water, and it got bent while I was still young." Another woman said to me, "You know, I swore I would never be bent like my mother, and then I got married, and the first time I had to do the wash I knew I was going to look exactly like her by the time I was middle-aged."

To show me—the city boy—what washdays were like without electricity, these women would get out their old big "Number 3" zinc washtubs and line them up—three of them— on the lawn, as they had once done every Monday. Next to them they'd build a fire, and they would put a huge vat of boiling water over it.

A woman would put her clothes into the first wash-tub and wash them by bending over the washboard. Back in those days they couldn't afford "store-bought" soap, so they would use soap made of lye. "Do you know what it's like to use lye soap all day?" they'd ask me. "Well, that soap would strip the skin off your hands like it was a glove." Then they'd shift the clothes to the vat of boiling water and try to get out the rest of the dirt by "punching" the clothes with a broom handle—standing there and swirling them around like the agitator in a washing machine. Then they'd shift the clothes to the second zinc washtub—the rinsing tub —and finally to the bluing tub.

The clothes would be shifted from tub to tub by lifting them out on the end of a broomstick. These old women would say to me, "You're from the city—I bet you don't know how heavy a load of wet clothes on the end of a broomstick is. Here, feel it." And I did—and in that moment I understood more about what electricity had meant to the Hill Country and why the people loved the man who brought it. A dripping load of soggy clothes on the end of a broomstick is heavy. Each load had to be moved on that broomstick from one washtub to the other. For the average Hill Country farm family, a week's wash consisted of eight loads. And for each load, of course, the women had to go back to the well and haul more water on her yoke. And all this effort was in addition to bending all day over the "rubboards." Lyndon's cousin, Ava, who still lives in Johnson City, told me one day, "By the time you got done washing, your back was broke. I'll tell you—of the things in my life that I will never forget, I will never forget how my back hurt on washdays." Hauling the water, scrubbing, punching the clothes, rinsing: a Hill Country wife did this for hours on end; a city wife did it by pressing the button on her electric washing machine.

Tuesday was ironing day. Well, I don't intend to take you through the entire week here, but I'll never forget the shock it was for me to learn how hard it was to iron in a kitchen over a wood stove, where you have to keep throwing the wood on to keep the temperature hot all day. The irons—heavy slabs of metal—weighed seven or eight pounds, and a Hill Country housewife would have four or five of them heating all day. In the Hill Country it's nothing for the temperature to be 100 or even 105 degrees, and those kitchens would be like an oven. The women of the Hill Country called their irons the "sad irons." I came to understand why.

I came to realize that the man I was writing about had grown up in an area that was a century and more behind the rest of America where life was mostly a brutal drudgery. When Lyndon Johnson became congressman he promised the people of the Hill Country that he would bring them electricity. They elected him congressman, but nobody really believed that he could do it. For one thing, there was no source of hydroelectric power within hundreds of miles. A dam had been begun on the Lower Colorado River some years earlier, but the company that was building it had gone bankrupt in the Depression and its future was very uncertain. New federal financing was needed, and only the President could push that dam to completion. When Johnson got to Washington he became friends with Thomas Corcoran—"Tommy the Cork"—who was close to Roosevelt. And every time Johnson saw Corcoran he would say, "The next time you see the President, remind him about my dam." And Corcoran reminded Roosevelt so often that finally one day Roosevelt said in exasperation, "Oh, give the kid the dam."

Once the dam was built, there was a source of electric power, but there still seemed no feasible way of getting this power out to the people. The Rural Electrification Administration had minimum density standards—about five persons per square mile, I think it was—and they said, "We're not going to lay thousands and thousands of miles of wire to connect one family here and another family over there." And the story of how Lyndon Johnson persuaded the REA to do this—how he circumvented through his ingenuity not only the REA but dozens of government agencies and regulations and brought the people electricity—is one of the most dramatic and noble examples of the use of government that I have ever heard. Actually it took more than ten years—it was 1948 before some of the people got electricity. But they did get it, and the men I talked to who had worked on the line-laying crews would tell me how they never had to bring lunch because the farm families were so grateful. When they saw the crews coming, stretching that precious wire toward them across the hills, they would set tables outside, with their best linen and dishes, to welcome the men.

And all over the Hill Country, people began to name their children after Lyndon Johnson. This one man had changed the lives of more than one hundred thousand people—had brought them, literally by himself, into the twentieth century, and when Tommy Corcoran said to me, shortly before he died, "Lyndon Johnson was the best congressman for a district that ever *was*," I knew exactly what he meant.

At every stage of his life Lyndon Johnson revealed this genius for government. In 1933, before he was a congressman, when he was only a twenty-four-year-old secretary to another congressman, in the midst of the Depression, many farms were being foreclosed. Roosevelt had signed legislation creating the Federal Land Bank shortly after his inauguration. This occurred on a Friday, but on the next Tuesday the sheriff of Nueces County was going to nail up on the county courthouse the foreclosure notices on sixty-seven homes. It seemed that this legislation couldn't be used to help these farmers because they were simply too far behind in their payments for it to help them—certainly not by Tuesday. Between Friday afternoon and Tuesday, Lyndon Johnson had to devise a formula whereby the legislation could be made to apply to this type of farm that was so deeply in arrears. He had to persuade the seven governors of the Federal Land Bank board to accept this formula, and he had to have them order the local supervisors and appraisers out to the farms, and he did it all. By that Tuesday—actually on the Monday night before—these sixty-seven farmers had their homes saved.

At the age of twenty-six Johnson was director of the National Youth Administration, the youngest director of such an agency in the United States and probably the best. The men who worked for him would tell me how he inspired them, how he would stand there and tell them that the idea was to get kids to go back to school or to stay in college by giving them jobs. He would say, "Put 'em to work, get 'em off the streets. Put 'em to work, get 'em out of the boxcars." One man who worked for him, Willard Deason, said, "Days made no difference to him, nights made no difference. Weekdays and weekends made no difference. All we'd do is work. And thinking back on it, I see that he made us do the impossible."

So we see the seeds of the Great Society in the young Lyndon Johnson.

Unfortunately, that's not all we see. There existed in the career and personality of Lyndon Johnson a dark side that is as dark as the other side is bright. We can see it in terms of his district, and we can see it in terms of Roosevelt. As good a congressman as Johnson was for the district, all he wanted to do with that congressional seat, from the day he got in it, was to get out of it and move up to his next step, which was the Senate. He tried to do that as soon as possible. He ran for the Senate just four years after his election to the House. He lost, but ran again in 1948 and won. And to win he switched sides completely. Texas at that time was dominated by oil interests and natural gas and sulphur interests. Their concern with government—state and national—was to make sure that government didn't interfere with them on behalf of the people. The payment of even a very small share of the billions of dollars they were taking out of the state's soil would have enabled the state's government to improve greatly the lot of the state's people. But they didn't want to pay any taxes at all. These men were reactionaries. They hated the working man, they hated the labor unions, they hated the blacks, they hated the Jews. And they hated Franklin Roosevelt.

Lyndon Johnson adopted their philosophy and their positions. He allied himself with them, and in return for their support he made himself their willing tool. The methods he used are not pleasant even to discuss. Betrayal was one of them. He betrayed Roosevelt. Roosevelt had helped him more than he had helped any other young politician. When Johnson came to the conclusion that Roosevelt couldn't help him with his greater ambitions, he turned against Roosevelt in an instant.

Much sadder was his betrayal of Sam Rayburn. When people ask me, "What's the most unpleasant thing you found out when you were doing your book? What was the most unpleasant part of your research?" I never have any trouble knowing what it was. It was when I found out what Lyndon Johnson did to Sam Rayburn.

Today Sam Rayburn, the great Speaker of the House

of Representatives, is getting lost to history, which is a shame. But for two decades he ruled the House of Representatives as no man ruled it before or since. Rayburn was a uniquely honest man. He never wrote memos for the record; he never wrote memos to himself. Someone once asked him, after a long day in the House of Representatives, "How do you remember all the things you promised people?" Rayburn replied, "If you always tell the truth, you don't need memos to remember what you said."

I came to appreciate Rayburn's power, but I also came to appreciate his loneliness. He very much wanted a wife and children. He didn't have them. He once wrote to his sister, "God, what I would give for a tow-headed boy to take fishing!" During the week, of course, Rayburn would be surrounded by people—assistants, other congressmen, favor-seekers—in the House, but when the House adjourned for the day, the other people went home to their families. On weekends Rayburn was alone. He used to go for long walks all through Washington every weekend, roaming all over the city, with his face set in that grim look that we remember so well, as if daring anyone to talk to him, as if he wanted to be alone—because he never wanted to let anyone know how lonely he was. One of the last of the aides who knew the Speaker during this era told me how sometimes, driven by loneliness, Mr. Sam would telephone him at home on a Sunday and gruffly order him to come to his office in the Capitol, as if he had some urgent job for him. The assistant would go there and he'd watch Mr. Sam pulling open the drawers of his desk, one after the other, looking for something he could give the assistant to do.

When Lyndon and Lady Bird Johnson came to Washington they made themselves Sam Rayburn's family. Once, talking of "The Speaker," Mrs. Johnson said: "He was the best of *us*—the best of simple American people." She truly loved Rayburn. She learned to cook his favorite foods—chili and cornbread and homemade peach ice cream—the way he liked them. And every Sunday Rayburn would come to the Johnsons' apartment, and after breakfast Lady Bird would clear away the dishes and the two men would sit there with the Sunday papers, talking. Johnson played on Rayburn's loneliness, and Rayburn came to depend on him. Rayburn was also like a father to him. Once, when Johnson was about twenty-six, Lady Bird was back in Texas on a vacation, and Lyndon came down with a serious case of pneumonia and was taken to the hospital. Sam Rayburn sat next to his bed, all night in a straight chair, in the hospital, chain-smoking cigarettes. And because he was afraid to disturb Lyndon if he was sleeping, he didn't move, not even to stand up and brush away the cigarette ashes. In the morning, when Johnson awoke, Rayburn was sitting there with his lapels and his vest covered with ashes. And when he saw that Johnson was awake, Rayburn leaned over and said, "Now, Lyndon, don't you worry. Take it easy. If you ever need anything, call on me."

Only a few months later Johnson did call on him. Roosevelt was creating the National Youth Administration, and Johnson wanted to be its Texas state director. Of course his first overtures to the White House were greeted with ridicule. He was only twenty-six years old. He was just a secretary to a congressman. Who would make him the head of a multimillion-dollar federal agency? Sam Rayburn had the reputation in Washington of never asking a man for a favor. But he went to Tom Connally, the old senator from Texas, and he asked Connally to use his patronage powers to have Lyndon Johnson appointed. In his memoirs Connally wrote, "It was an astonishing thing. Rayburn would not leave my office until I agreed to do it." And as a result Johnson was appointed and his political career was on its way.

But there came a point, just a few years later, when Roosevelt needed a man in Texas. The man who had run the state for him, Vice-President John Garner, was feuding with him. Only one man was going to have the power of the New Deal in Texas, the power to dispense its patronage and its contracts, and the logical choice was Rayburn, who was then majority leader of the House. So Johnson had to turn Roosevelt against

Rayburn. And he did. No one was more loyal to Roosevelt than Sam Rayburn; in fact, when we look at so many of the bills that we've come to associate with the New Deal, they never would have been passed if Rayburn hadn't used his prestige and his political genius to get them through the House of Representatives. Johnson, by deceiving Roosevelt, made him believe that Rayburn was in fact his enemy. And Johnson became Roosevelt's man in Texas.

Now, learning about this dark side of Lyndon Johnson was, as I've said, not at all pleasant. I'll never forget learning about his betrayal of Rayburn. You never learn about a thing like that from just one document. But when you're sitting there in the Johnson Library, which has thirty-two million documents, if you keep reading enough of them you'll eventually come across almost everything. And gradually, as I was going through the intra-office memos, and the telephone calls and the telegrams from many different files, I began to see unfolding what had happened between Roosevelt and Rayburn and the role Lyndon Johnson had played in it. I can still remember my feeling, which was: "God, I hope this doesn't mean what I think it does." But in fact, as the memos and the letters continued and as I went to the people who were still alive who had written those memos and who could explain them, they did mean exactly what they had seemed to mean, and the story was just as sordid as I had feared it would be.

The major problem in writing about Lyndon Johnson's early life was his desire for secrecy and concealment. He had a unique talent for it. I don't think many people would have gone to the trouble, as he did, of having pages of his college yearbook, which detailed unsavory episodes in his college career, cut out with a razor blade from hundreds of copies of the yearbook. The nation saw this obsession with secrecy when Johnson was President, but, again, it went all the way back. A young man who worked for him when he was secretary to a congressman had been one of his students when Johnson was a high school teacher, and this man told me that after Johnson went to Washington he would write him the normal letters that a teacher writes back to the kids he has been teaching, but on each letter Johnson would write, "Burn this." I asked what was in the letters, and he said, "Nothing significant. They were just casual letters, but he always wanted them burned. And he wasn't kidding, because the next time he'd see you the first thing he'd ask was, 'Did you burn those letters?'" I didn't believe that, and I wasn't prepared to put it in my book until finally this man found a letter with "Burn this!" written on it and showed it to me.

When Ina and I moved up to the Hill Country and

people realized that I was there to stay—that I wasn't just one more reporter coming through for a month and then going back to write the definitive work on what the Hill Country was like—they started talking more frankly. And they started to tell me the true story of Lyndon Johnson's college career and indeed of his entire youth. It was a story very much different from the one that had been printed in previous biographies and in thousands of magazine and newspaper articles, and for quite some time I really didn't believe what they were telling me. I still remember spending a long afternoon with one of Johnson's college classmates, a man named Henry Kyle, who told me a sordid and amazing story about how Johnson at college had begun stealing elections, about how he won one campus election by using against a young woman what his lieutenants called "blackmail," about how Johnson was so widely mistrusted that he was called by a classmate "a man who just could not tell the truth." I always try to type my interview notes up the same day, so that all the nuances will still be fresh in my mind, but I didn't bother typing this interview because I thought it was probably not true but only the recollections of an envious and embittered college rival. In fact, it turned out to be completely true.

Lyndon Johnson was a great storyteller, vivid and persuasive, and he told stories that were repeated over and over again, in books and articles, thousands of times. He really created his own legend. And the legend isn't true. I'll never forget the day I first found that out for sure. Before that I had been getting a lot of hints about it. Lyndon Johnson died at the age of sixty-four, and when I started my research he would have been only sixty-seven, so most of the people who went to school and college with him and participated in his early career were still alive. Indeed, many of them, when I first arrived in Johnson City, were still living there, some of them on the very same street on which they had grown up.

When I began talking to these people, I would, in an attempt to get more details, more color, repeat the stories that had become the legend of Lyndon Johnson's youth, the legend he had created. At this point I really had no idea that they weren't true. But the people would say, "Well, some of that didn't really happen, you know," or "Well, there's more to it than that, but I don't want to tell you what it is—you shouldn't tell bad things about a President." I began to get the feeling that something was drastically and basically wrong with the legend, but I didn't really pick up on what they were trying to tell me.

One day, however, I did the following thing. I had already interviewed Lyndon Johnson's brother four or five times, but the interviews were very unproductive, or, to be more exact, they were very unreliable. In the first place Sam Houston Johnson drank a lot.

He also talked with a bravado that m
distrustful of what he said. And whe~
check out the various stories that he ι.
often they weren't true. I decided not to use anyι.
that he had told me. One day, however, perhaps two
or three years after I had stopped interviewing him, I
met Sam Houston in the streets of Johnson City, and
I saw a changed man. During the interim he had had
cancer and had had at least one terrible operation.
And he had stopped drinking. But more than that,
when you talked to him, he was calmer. He had become very religious, and he was just a calmer, more
serious kind of man. And I decided to try him again.

Now, the National Park Service has re-created Lyndon Johnson's boyhood home in Johnson City.
They've done a very good job of it, according to his
relatives, and it looks pretty much the way it did when
Lyndon and Sam Houston were growing up. So it was
arranged that I would bring Sam there after the tourists
had left for the day. And when we were there all alone,
I said, "Now, Sam Houston, sit down in your seat at
the dinner table." They had this long dining-room
table. And the three sisters would sit on one side, and
Lyndon and Sam would sit on the other, and the father
and the mother were at the two ends. And I said, "I
want you to re-create for me one of those terrible argu-
ments that your father used to have at this table with
Lyndon." I wanted to put him back in his boyhood—

to make him remember accurately how things had happened. At first it was very slow going. I'd have to ask, "Well, then, what would your father say?" and then, "What would Lyndon say?" But gradually the inhibitions fell away, and it was no longer necessary for me to say anything. He started talking faster and faster. And finally he was shouting back and forth—the father, for example, shouting, "Lyndon, God damn it, you're a failure, you'll be a failure all your life." By this time I felt that he was really in the frame to remember accurately, and I said, "Now, Sam Houston, I want you to tell me all the stories about your brother's boyhood that you told me before, the stories that your brother told all those years, only give me more details." There was this long pause. Then he said, "I can't." I said, "Why not?" And he said, "Because they never happened."

And in fact, as you can see in my book, they didn't happen. Sam Houston started from the beginning and told me a completely different story of Lyndon Johnson's youth—one that cast an entirely new and different and significant light on that youth, and on the character of this man who became President. And this time, when I went back to the people who were involved in these incidents, they remembered and confirmed them. Lyndon Johnson tried to write his own legend for history, and he almost succeeded. If I hadn't been lucky enough to come along when his brother and his sister and his boyhood companions and his college classmates and early political associates were still alive, that legend would have gone down in history.

Well, now I'm writing the second and third volumes of the Johnson biography. They deal with more public, one might say more historically significant, matters: his rise to power in the Senate (in an institution in which previously only seniority mattered, he became his party's leader just four years after he got there); how he achieved passage, against incredible odds, of the first Civil Rights Act in 1957 (no one but LBJ could have done that, in my opinion); his blood feud with the Kennedys, which is a drama of Shakespearean vividness; then the Presidency; the Great Society, Vietnam, the whole, great surging and heaving panorama of the turbulent sixties. Doing the work on these next two volumes is constantly interesting. But although the work takes me to Austin, to the Johnson Library, and to other parts of Texas, and to Washington and to other states to interview former Senators and cabinet members, the one place it never seems to take me is back to the Hill Country. And to tell the truth, even when I'm back here in New York, enjoying myself, I frequently find myself missing the Hill Country very much.

Well, I tried to keep this speech short, shorter than I have, but if I could keep things short I guess I wouldn't always be writing nine-hundred-page books.

———

Q. What motivated you to choose Lyndon Johnson as a subject?

A. I was never interested in writing biographies merely to tell the lives of famous men. I never had the slightest interest in doing that. From the first time I thought of becoming a biographer, I conceived of biography as a means of illuminating the times and the great forces that shape the times—particularly political power. A biography will only do that, of course, if the biography is of the right man.

Why am I so interested in political power? Because in a democracy, political power shapes all our lives. You can see this in simple, small, relatively insignificant things. Robert Moses, the subject of my first biography, *The Power Broker,* agreed to put the Manhattan terminus of his Triborough Bridge at 125th Street instead of 96th Street, as had been planned and as was more convenient and logical, because William Randolph Hearst, the influential publisher, owned real estate on 125th Street and he wanted it condemned for the bridge. Every time you drive twenty-nine blocks out of your way to get to the Triborough Bridge your life is being affected—in a small way, of course—by political power as exercised by Robert Moses.

This is a very minor example. But there are very big, significant examples, too. Every time a youth from a poor family gets to go to college because of one of Lyndon Johnson's Great Society programs, and thus to escape from a life in the ghetto, and every time a black man or woman is able to walk into a voting booth and cast a vote because of one of Lyndon Johnson's Voting Rights Acts, that is a more significant example of political power. And so, unfortunately, is the fact of a young man dying a needless death in a useless war in Vietnam.

In order to demonstrate and illuminate political power through a biography of a single individual, the biography has to be of the right individual. I selected Robert Moses because in *The Power Broker* what I was aiming at was to show how urban political power worked in America in the middle of the twentieth century—how power worked not just in New York, but in all our great cities; to show what was the true essence of urban political power, not the trappings but the heart, the raw, naked essence of such power. I selected Moses because he was never elected to anything. But for forty-four years he exercised more power in New York City and State than any official who *was* elected —more than any mayor, more than any governor. Therefore, I felt, if I could show what Moses' power consisted of, and how he got it and how he wielded it, I would be showing the true essence of urban political power. Since no one else ever wielded such power, Moses was the ideal subject.

I selected Lyndon Johnson as my next subject because I wanted to attempt to do the same thing with national political power. What first attracted me to Johnson as a subject was not his Presidency but his time as Senate Majority Leader. When he was Leader it was said of him that no Leader in history ever controlled, dominated, the Senate as he did. So I felt, if I could show how he did that, I would be showing the essence, the heart, of national political power. Now I don't say I succeeded in doing these things, but that is what I wanted to do. With Lyndon Johnson, in the second and third volumes, that is what I am still trying to do.

Q. How did you go about approaching the people in the Hill Country for interviews, before they knew who you were and what you were doing?

A. It was very hard, because I'm a New Yorker and I don't look like someone from the Hill Country. But more than that, the problem was their experience with previous journalists and some writers of other books. These people had a lot of pride in the Hill Country. They loved their land, and over and over writers would come down and spend a week or a month there, and then go back and write all about how Johnson City was, pretending to an understanding that nobody could possibly acquire in a week or a month. The people felt—and they were right—that they were being used, and that the things that were being written didn't accurately reflect the country they loved. When we moved there, as soon as I said, "I love it here and I'm going to live here, and I'm going to stay here as long as it takes to truly understand it," their attitude really changed. My wife, Ina, played a very important role, especially in those chapters relating to electricity. She played a very important role in other parts of the book also. In the chapters about electricity it was particularly important because many of these women didn't want to talk to me at first. They're women from other generations who are now quite elderly. They are very shy to a degree that's hard for people from New York even to understand. It's another world, in the more remote and isolated areas down there. Ina was terrific in winning their confidence and explaining to them how I had to learn all the different aspects of doing the washing and the ironing.

Q. What has the reaction been to the first volume of your book?

A. The reaction in the Hill Country is a phrase that I heard over and over. My phone would ring and it would be some person from the Hill Country, and they'd say, "You got him right on the head!"

Q. What is your relationship to the Johnson family?

A. Mrs. Johnson was very helpful to me in the early years of my research. I spent a great deal of time with her—nine interviews, some of them quite extensive. Some time before the book came out she decided not to cooperate anymore.

Q. You mentioned that you went through thirty-two million documents in the Johnson Library. How is this possible?

A. Well, I didn't mean to imply that I was going to look at all thirty-two million documents. I once figured it out, and you couldn't do it in a lifetime. For the first volume it was possible for me to try to look at most of the papers that related to that period. It was manageable. I don't know how many months, or indeed years, I spent in the library there. I once figured it was about two years just going through papers. For the next two volumes I have to be more selective in my research.

But I don't want to be too selective. Because you can find valuable material in those papers in very unlikely places. For example, campaign contributions and how Lyndon Johnson used cash to finance his rise to power. I was told about that, almost in the first week I was working on the book, because one of the first people I went to see was Tommy Corcoran. He was a very blunt old guy, a great political mind, and a great political manipulator. He and I really hit it off; he always used to call me "Kid" for some reason. In one of our very first talks I said, "I don't understand how Lyndon Johnson got power so *fast*," and he said, "Money, kid. Money."

But he also said, "You're never going to be able to write about that." I said, "Why not?" And he said, "Because you'll never find anything in writing." Well, Mr. Corcoran was correct in saying that I couldn't have written about Johnson's methods—for example, what he did in 1940, when he used the campaign contributions from Texas oilmen to finance the campaigns of other congressmen, which is how he built his first national power base—without finding written documentation. And for a long time—several years, as I recall it —I thought he was also correct in saying that I would never find any such documentation. But then one day, while I was sitting in the Johnson Library looking through files that supposedly dealt with some totally unrelated subject, suddenly there it was: the intra-office memos: Congressman So-and-So needs $1,500. Congressman So-and-So needs so much money. The frantic telegrams from the congressmen themselves. "Lyndon, help! Need $2,000 immediately." And the telegrams from the Texas contractors and oilmen who were sending the money to be given to the congressmen through Johnson. George Brown is sending $30,-000. $5,000 arriving from Sid Richardson tonight. Whatever. And in the margins, next to the congressman's requests, Lyndon Johnson would write, "O.K." or "Give 500," or "none." That sort of thing. So it really is necessary to look at as much material as you can.

Q. Since you're writing about power as much as you're writing about an individual, do you think it's necessary to stick to strict chronology?

A. In the case of the two men I've been writing about —first Robert Moses and now Lyndon Johnson—I think it's absolutely vital to stick to strict chronology because they were so devious. Things they did that you can't understand if you try to take them as isolated decisions suddenly become very clear if you just make yourself take one thing after another. Then you see what the person was doing. Dumas Malone wrote the definitive explanation of that in connection with Jefferson—about how Jefferson's mystery falls away if you'll just follow him through life the way he went through life—chronologically.

Q. During the Presidency, Lady Bird seems like a much stronger and more assertive person than the picture you draw in your book. Why is that?

A. That's correct. She became a stronger and more assertive person. In fact, the transformation occurs right at the beginning of the second volume because the first volume ends at the time of Pearl Harbor. When World War II is declared, Lyndon Johnson gets a commission as a lieutenant commander and goes off to the Pacific. Mrs. Johnson has to run his congressional office. Mrs. Johnson had never done anything of this kind. She was a timid, shy woman who wouldn't even dream of making a speech for her husband in a campaign. She was often not in the room if they were talking about politics. "I didn't always want to be a part of everything," she told me. How she transformed herself, by strength of will, into a woman who could run a congressional office and a radio station is one of the most dramatic stories I've ever heard, and I've tried to tell it in detail in the second volume.

Q. How well educated was Lyndon Johnson? Was he a reader?

A. He certainly wasn't a reader. The small number of books that he read in his entire life after college is quite astonishing. His education, which was not his fault, was terrible. He went to San Marcos, which was then a little college in the Hill Country whose level I would compare to my last year of high school. He was very poorly educated, and he felt it. But he also did nothing to try to remedy it.

Bibliography
Contributors

Bibliography

When we were planning this lecture series, it occurred to us that we would like to know what sources our six authors consulted when they were writing their books. We asked them if they would give us an informal list of the works they had found most useful, or most memorable, or most engaging—books pertaining to the person or the family they were writing about, or to the field or the period or the locale, or to the process of writing biography—and to tell us why.

This bibliography is their answer to our request. Though it covers the entire series, it was given to everyone who came to any of the six lectures. Our feeling was that biography has an appeal that goes beyond its particular subject. Biographers are a dogged breed, tracking down and piecing together countless scraps of fact and recollection, and the pleasure is in seeing how they go about their search, first poking down trails taken by previous scholars and then breaking out into terrain where nobody else has gone.

DAVID McCULLOUGH

The best-known and best books on Harry Truman are nearly all autobiographical in spirit:

Memoirs, by Harry S. Truman (Doubleday, 1955), is HST's own account of his Presidency in two volumes. It's filled with personality and momentous history and not enough of his early life. Like most autobiographies, it's also interesting in what it leaves out.

Plain Speaking, by Merle Miller (Berkley, 1973), has probably had more to do with the present popular impression of HST than anything ever published. A salty, elderly, down-home Truman talks on tape about himself and the world at large, and nearly all of it is extremely entertaining.

Off the Record: The Private Papers of Harry S. Truman, edited by Robert H. Ferrell (Harper and Row, 1980). HST poured himself out on paper with great vigor and candor all his life. This is a generous sample.

Dear Bess: The Letters from Harry to Bess Truman, 1910–1959, edited by Robert H. Ferrell (W. W. Norton, 1983). In what it reveals of his ambitions and inner turmoil, his humor and his sense of fair play, this collection is the most telling portrait we have of the prepresidential Truman.

Harry S. Truman, by Margaret Truman (William Morrow, 1972). A lively, well-written, often moving book that is also essentially autobiographical, since it's written from "the inside" by an adoring daughter.

Of the relative handful of biographies that have been written, my favorite is *The Man of Independence*, by Jonathan Daniels (J. B. Lippincott Co., 1950), which was published thirty-five years ago when HST was still in office. Daniels took the time to try to understand Truman's family background, and he had the advantage of knowing the man, but he too was an insider—he served on HST's White House staff—and so the book has some of the failings of an authorized biography.

The most comprehensive study of the Truman Presidency is by Robert J. Donovan, who as a Washington correspondent witnessed much of the history he writes about. *Conflict and Crisis* (W. W. Norton, 1977) begins with FDR's death in 1945 and ends with the upset election of 1948; *The Tumultuous Years* (W. W. Norton, 1982) covers 1949 through 1953.

For accounts of the Truman years by some of the protagonists, I like especially *Speaking Frankly*, by James F. Byrnes (Harper & Bros. 1947); *The Forrestal Diaries* (Viking, 1951); and Dean Acheson's brilliant *Present at the Creation* (W. W. Norton, 1969).

There is a good chapter on Truman in *Through These Men*, by John Mason Brown (Harper & Bros., 1956).

Bibliography

For a wonderfully deft sketch of HST as he goes about his business within the White House, read John Hersey's *Aspects of the Presidency* (Ticknor & Fields, 1980).

And for a vivid, entertaining reminder of just how low some opinion of Truman went, back when he wasn't a distant memory, there is *The Truman Merry-Go-Round*, by Robert S. Allen and William V. Shannon (Vanguard, 1950). The portrayal of the Truman "cronies" is memorable.

As for the subject of biography and the problems of writing biography, I don't suppose there is anything better than Catherine Drinker Bowen's *Biography: The Craft and the Calling* (Little, Brown & Co., 1969). But the books on writing that I've gotten the most from are Paul Horgan's *Approaches to Writing* (Farrar, Straus and Giroux, 1968), the first *Paris Review* anthology of interviews with writers, and W. Somerset Maugham's *The Summing Up* (Doubleday, 1938; Penguin, 1978).

I'm also fond of a line I found in the autobiography of the famous American surgeon of the last century Samuel D. Gross: "The only way to write well is to be thoroughly acquainted with one's subject."

RICHARD B. SEWALL

When I started out on this biography, Millicent Todd Bingham, then the high priestess of Dickinson studies (if such they could be called then), told me: "There is just so much primary material: the *Poems*, the *Letters*, Jay Leyda, and *Home*." By which she meant Emily Dickinson's poems and letters, handsomely edited by Thomas H. Johnson (Harvard University Press, 1955 and 1958); Jay Leyda's *The Years and Hours of Emily Dickinson* (Yale University Press, 1960), and her own *Emily Dickinson's Home: Letters of Edward Dickinson and His Family* (Harper & Bros., 1955). Then she added, with emphasis: "*All the rest is conjecture.*"

This was a challenge, I saw, to stick to the facts, to the evidence, to documents. Avoid the clichés: the Nun of Amherst, the Frustrated Lover, the Ogre Father, et cetera. Don't fictionalize her, don't impose patterns, don't "reduce" her—e.g., Rebecca Patterson, *The Riddle of Emily Dickinson* (Houghton Mifflin, 1951)—the lesbian conjecture; John Evangelist Walsh, *The Hidden Life of Emily Dickinson* (Simon & Schuster, 1971)— the plagiarist conjecture; Clark Griffith, *The Long Shadow* (Princeton

University Press, 1964)—the father theory; John Cody, *After Great Pain: The Inner Life of Emily Dickinson* (Harvard University Press, 1971)—the mother theory.

Recently, too late for my purposes, the feminists have swung into action: Sandra Gilbert and Susan Gubar, *The Madwoman in the Attic* (Yale University Press, 1979)—the final section; Sharon Cameron, *Lyric Time: Dickinson and the Limits of Gender* (Johns Hopkins Press, 1979); Vivian Pollack, *Dickinson: The Anxiety of Gender* (Cornell University Press, 1984). They paint Emily Dickinson as a woman chafing under the limitations imposed by her sex; Emily herself might be surprised at the number of poems in which they find rage. A good antidote, itself controversial, is Karl Keller's *The Only Kangaroo Among the Beauty* (Johns Hopkins Press, 1979). The book starts with Anne Bradstreet and cites her life as a model for those who would understand Emily Dickinson.

As for criticism, these helped me most:

Anderson, Charles. *Emily Dickinson's Poetry: Stairway of Surprise* (Holt, Rinehart & Winston, 1960). Some brilliant explication of individual poems.

Kher, Inder Nath. *Landscape of Absence* (Yale University Press, 1974). Shows Dickinson's affinities with main currents of modern thought, worldwide.

Miller, Ruth. *The Poetry of Emily Dickinson* (Wesleyan University Press, 1966). Focuses on Dickinson's failures to get published—but always powerfully.

Porter, David. *The Art of Emily Dickinson's Early Poetry* (Harvard University Press, 1966). Expert analysis.

Wells, Henry W. *Introduction to Emily Dickinson* (Hendrick's House, 1947).

Whicher, George. *This Was a Poet* (Scribners, 1938). The pioneer study.

Studies of Emily Dickinson have proliferated since my book was published in 1974. See especially:

Benfey, Christopher E. G. *Emily Dickinson and the Problem of Others* (University of Massachusetts Press, 1984). The first book that gives Dickinson philosophical status, along with Emerson and Thoreau.

Porter, David. *Dickinson: The Modern Idiom* (Harvard University Press, 1981). The first half brilliant and convincing, the last half brilliant—and controversial.

[238

Weisbuch, Robert. *Emily Dickinson's Poetry* (University of Chicago Press, 1972).

There are many other studies, of course. In fact, every month seems to bring an announcement of a new one. Which shows that Emily Dickinson is at last receiving the recognition that, forty years ago, would have seemed incredible.

PAUL C. NAGEL

As a person interested in biography and history, I have found these three books both delightful and useful:

Bowen, Catherine Drinker. *Adventures of a Biographer* (Little, Brown & Co., 1959).

Bowen, Catherine Drinker. *Biography: The Craft and the Calling* (Little, Brown & Co., 1969).

Tuchman, Barbara W. *Practicing History* (Alfred A. Knopf, 1981).

In these books, two of the most successful writers and biographers of this century talk about how and why they work.

My favorite biographies are:

Freeman, Douglas Southall. *R. E. Lee, A Biography*, 4 vols. (Scribners, 1934).

Malone, Dumas. *Jefferson and His Times*, 6 vols. (Little, Brown & Co., 1948–81).

Mattingly, Garrett. *Catherine of Aragon* (Little, Brown & Co., 1941).

Miller, Perry. *Jonathan Edwards* (W. Sloane Associates, 1949; University of Massachusetts Press, 1981).

Each of these biographers has his own subject and style, but all of them represent an older biographical tradition that I admire. These writers composed their books out of a lifetime of study, yet they are such masters of the biographer's art that the size and the erudition of their work simply enlarge the opportunity for their reader's enjoyment.

Because I am now fascinated by women as a subject for biography, I find the following two authors to be dependable guides:

Degler, Carl. *At Odds: Women and the Family in America from the Revolution to the Present* (Oxford University Press, 1980).

Gay, Peter. *The Bourgeois Experience: From Victoria to Freud,* vol. 1, *Education of the Senses* (Oxford University Press, 1984).

Each volume is an excellent example of how today's scholarship assists the biographer in understanding the inner life of women. It remains to be seen whether books by men can do this to a superior degree, but these two volumes are encouraging evidence.

Among the many books published recently in family history, I find these to be especially enjoyable:

Bleser, Carol. *The Hammonds of Redcliffe* (Oxford University Press, 1981).

Longsworth, Polly. *Austin and Mabel* (Holt, Rinehart & Winston, 1985).

Matthiessen, F. O. *The James Family* (Alfred A. Knopf, 1947).

Middlekauff, Robert. *The Mathers* (Oxford University Press, 1971).

Myers, Robert Manson. *The Children of Pride* (Yale University Press, 1972).

This list includes families from across America, with stories that are as varied as the approaches of the different writers. Each book is strengthened by a skilled blending of excerpts from family letters, which complement the biographer's thoughtful interpretation.

My favorite books about members of the Adams family are:

Bemis, Samuel F. *John Quincy Adams and the Foundations of American Foreign Policy* (Alfred A. Knopf, 1949) and *John Quincy Adams and the Union* ("S. F. Bemis" is the by-line used in this book; Alfred A. Knopf, 1956) are beautifully written studies that have the advantage of early work in the Adams family papers. Bemis acknowledges that he was reluctant to probe the personal life and character of his subject. That remains a challenge to some future biographer.

Butterfield, L. H., Marc Friedlaender, and Mary Jo Kline (eds.). *The Book of Abigail and John* (Harvard University Press, 1975). A skillfully guided tour through some of the best letters exchanged by these wonderful correspondents.

Donald, David and Aida (eds.). *Diary of Charles Francis Adams,* 2 vols. (Harvard University Press, 1964). Taylor, Robert J., et al. *Diary of John Quincy Adams,* 2 vols. (Harvard University Press, 1981). These volumes are from the youthful diaries of two great Americans. Any lover of biography will be fascinated by these detailed and candid disclosures of young manhood in the early republic.

Levenson, J. C. and others (eds.). *The Letters of Henry Adams*, 3 vols. (Harvard University Press, 1982). These volumes, which extend from 1858 to 1892, contain some of the most delightful letters written by an American. They are well edited, leaving the casual reader easily absorbed in the life, humor, and ideas of America's greatest man of letters.

Samuels, Ernest. *The Young Henry Adams* (Harvard University Press, 1948); *Henry Adams: The Middle Years* (Harvard University Press, 1958); and *Henry Adams: The Major Phase* (Harvard University Press, 1964). ("E. Samuels" is the by-line used in the last two books.) In my opinion, this three-volume work constitutes one of the most readable scholarly biographies in our language. It has the advantage of being written by an author with an abiding interest in literature.

Smith, Page. *John Adams*, 2 vols. (Doubleday, 1962). This is the first biography to succeed in showing that John and Abigail were more complex personalities than history perceived them to be.

Withey, Lynne. *Dearest Friend* (Free Press, 1981). The best biography of Abigail Adams but somewhat diminished by the hastening to make Abigail a feminist model. Biographers must resist this temptation if we are to know Abigail Adams well.

RONALD STEEL

Walter Lippmann himself was such a superb stylist and fresh thinker that one is almost tempted to say that his own books are the best that one could read on the subject. I will resist that temptation only partially.

The two books he wrote when he was in his early twenties, *A Preface to Politics* (M. Kennerly, 1913) and *Drift & Mastery* (M. Kennerly, 1914; Prentice-Hall, 1961), give a real sense of a supple mind, endowed with a fine prose style, testing itself against the world. They are still a delight. A selection of his editorials for the *New Republic*, written between 1914 and 1921, compiled under the title *Early Writings* (Liveright, 1970), show the extraordinary range of his interests—from imagist poetry to foreign policy—and are more revealing of his personality than almost anything he later wrote.

Lippmann's most important book—although the choice is not easy—is probably *Public Opinion* (Harcourt, Brace, and Company, 1922; Free Press, 1965), a "subversive" book (in John Dewey's phrase) that has affected the way we feel not only about the media's role in public life, but the very notion of democratic decision-making. His *A Preface to Morals* (Macmillan, 1929) is a touching effort to come to terms with morality in a world that had lost both its belief and its traditional values, while his *An Inquiry into the Principles of the Good Society* (Little, Brown & Co.) is no less relevant today in its examination of the role of government in men's lives than when he wrote it in 1937.

There have been a number of books about Lippmann, most of them by scholars and therefore more specialized than the general reader might like. In the bibliography of my Lippmann book I list the ones that I found the most rewarding. But I would single out two for special mention, each very different from the other.

The first is Charles Forcey's provocative study, *Crossroads of Liberalism: Croly, Weyl, Lippmann and the Progressive Era, 1900–1925* (Oxford University Press, 1961).

The other is Louis Auchincloss's wonderfully perceptive and engrossing novel *The House of the Prophet* (G. K. Hall, 1980), in which the Lippmann character is slightly disguised and scrupulously portrayed as a man dedicated, at all costs, to the pursuit of truth. This is a fascinating book that reveals a complex Lippmann no less "real" than my own, by one of our finest novelists, who knew him very well over a period of many years.

In addition, Richard Rovere, who first interested me in writing this biography, recounts his relationship with Lippmann in his own memoir, *Arrivals and Departures* (Macmillan, 1976).

Because my ignorance of Lippmann's times was very great, the books from which I learned were many and my debt is great. I will try to confine myself to just a few, lest the diligent reader become as enmeshed as I did in the unending fascination and complexity of our national life, from the lure of Manifest Destiny to the rude awakenings of Selma, Vietnam and Watergate.

Bibliography

Throughout my labors I relied greatly on Arthur Link's magisterial *American Epoch: A History of the United States Since the 1890s* (Alfred A. Knopf, 1967). There are a great many general histories of the United States, but I found none so thorough, reliable and sensible as this one. Henry F. May's *The End of American Innocence* (Alfred A. Knopf, 1959), a study of culture—social, literary and political—of the Progressive era, was so absorbing, graceful and yet scholarly that I nearly threw up my hands in despair at even daring to write anything that would cover the same time and material. It is a wonderful book.

I was in awe of, and learned immensely from, Henry Steele Commager's *The American Mind* (Yale University Press, 1950), a very great book by our greatest living historian. I was also stimulated, as an endless succession of history students have been, by Richard Hofstadter's collection of presidential portraits, *The American Political Tradition* (Alfred A. Knopf, 1951), which shows that one can be both learned and provocative at the same time; by John Morton Blum's *The Republican Roosevelt* (Harvard University Press, 1954); and by Arthur Schlesinger, Jr.'s *The Age of Roosevelt: Crisis of the Old Order* (Houghton Mifflin, 1957), the first volume in his biographical study of Franklin D. Roosevelt.

Justin Kaplan's *Lincoln Steffens* (Simon & Schuster, 1974) taught me that a biography can be no less gripping than a novel, and Alfred Kazin's *On Native Grounds* (Reynal & Hitchcock, 1942) made me realize what an impossibly high standard I had set for myself. I recommend them all, and then I suggest that the reader return to the writings of Lippmann himself, who, now that his influence as a journalist is largely historic, still stands very high as a sensitive observer who, like Aristotle, saw politics at the very heart of the human condition.

JEAN STROUSE

BOOKS ABOUT THE JAMES FAMILY

Allen, Gay Wilson. *William James* (Viking Press, 1967). Allen's one-volume life of the philosopher and psychologist reads like a novel and brings the man himself very much alive.

Edel, Leon. *Henry James*, 5 vols. (J. B. Lippincott Co., 1953–1972). Edel's

243]

work, an invaluable resource for any toiler in the Jamesian fields, is one of the great literary biographies of the twentieth century. A revised and updated one-volume condensation was published in 1985.

James, Alice. *The Diary of Alice James*, edited with an introduction by Leon Edel (Dodd, Mead, and Co., 1964; Penguin, 1982). Though the diary covers only the last few years of Alice's life—1889–1892—it expresses fully her political acumen and lively curiosity, as well as her limitations and tyrannical invalidism.

James, Henry. Of particular biographical interest are his two books of autobiography, *A Small Boy and Others* and *Notes of a Son and Brother*, published in one volume as *Henry James Autobiography* (edited with an introduction by F. W. Dupee, Criterion Books, 1956), as well as the four volumes of letters (edited by Leon Edel and published by Harvard University Press, 1974–1984), and *The Notebooks of Henry James* (edited by F. O. Matthiessen and Kenneth B. Murdock, Oxford University Press, 1947). *The American Scene* (Horizon Press, 1967) is perennially interesting on everything from Sargent's portrait of Henry Lee Higginson and Newport before the Civil War to the American woman, the Tiffany building, and "the tepid South." Among the novels that have specific bearing on his sister's life (and vice versa) are *The Bostonians* and *The Princess Casamassima*, both published in 1886.

James, William. *The Principles of Psychology* (1890), *The Varieties of Religious Experience* (1902), *Pragmatism* (1907). James's elegant, original and energetic mind, exploring the nature of mind itself, proves surprisingly contemporary, and following his lead along these intellectual paths is a rare pleasure.

Matthiessen, F. O. *The James Family* (Alfred A. Knopf, 1947). Selections from the writings of Henry James, Sr., William James, Henry James, and Alice James. A unique family portrait, in which Matthiessen's artfully transparent narrative sets up each character's ideas, and places each individual in historical and literary context.

Perry, Ralph Barton. *The Thought and Character of William James*, 2 vols. (Little, Brown and Co., 1936). An old-fashioned, thoroughly enjoyable chronicle of the struggles and achievements in the life of a great man.

THE ART OF BIOGRAPHY

Pachter, Marc, ed. *Telling Lives* (New Republic Books, 1979). Subtitled *The Biographer's Art*, this excellent group of essays includes pieces by Justin Kaplan, Geoffrey Wolff, Leon Edel, Alfred Kazin, Doris Kearns, Theodore Rosengarten, and Barbara W. Tuchman. Pachter's introduction, surveying the field in the late twentieth century, begins with an epigraph from Strachey: "We do not reflect that it is perhaps as difficult to write a good life as to live one."

Scott, Geoffrey. *Portrait of Zélide* (Scribners, 1927). This eighteenth-century love story, featuring Madame de Charrière (Zélide) and Benjamin Constant, shows what magic a biographer can work with very limited sources. Using James Boswell, Madame de Staël, and the French Revolution as a backdrop for the captivating story of a pair of passionate, self-dramatizing lovers, Scott shows the changing climate of ideas in eighteenth-century Europe as it was experienced in private life. The book is out of print, a condition that some reprint house might want to correct.

Strachey, Lytton. *Eminent Victorians* (Chatto and Windus, 1918). Strachey's preface to these brilliant essays marked a sharp turn in the history of biography, from the exhaustive (and exhausting) chronicles of the nineteenth century to the more selective, interpretive approaches of the twentieth. Strachey begins: "The history of the Victorian Age will never be written: We know too much about it. For ignorance is the first requisite of the historian—ignorance, which simplifies and clarifies, which selects and omits, with a placid perfection unattainable by the highest art."

ROBERT A. CARO

In researching American history, I sometimes come across books that tell about fascinating characters who have been largely neglected by history, or that give new details about significant and dramatic events of which we know too little. Here are a few such books:

Allen, William H. *Al Smith's Tammany Hall* (The Institute for Public Service, 1958). The corrupt world that Smith sprang from and that he surmounted: Tammany Hall, chillingly detailed by a writer who hated corruption.

Alsop, Joseph, and Turner Catledge. *The 168 Days* (Doubleday, 1937). A little-known book, instructive in the depth of its detail, about the infighting between Franklin D. Roosevelt and the Senate over FDR's Supreme Court–packing plan. It contains as complete a description of Capitol Hill maneuvering as I've read, and a picture of some all-but-forgotten though fascinating political personalities, such as foxy old Cactus Jack Garner of Texas, the Roosevelt strategist Thomas (Tommy the Cork) Corcoran, the aristocratic Carter Glass of Virginia, and the profane Majority Leader Joe Robinson of Arkansas.

Croly, Herbert D. *Marcus Alonzo Hanna* (Macmillan, 1912). A tough cookie, vividly described.

Daniels, Jonathan. *Frontier on the Potomac* (Macmillan, 1946). Unusually fine as an evocation of the political atmosphere in wartime Washington.

Fowler, Gene. *Beau James* (Viking Press, 1949). "A Beau Brummel and a Guttersnipe" was what Robert Moses called Mayor Jimmy Walker. This book shows mostly the Beau Brummel side, but it is written in a tone that captures the man's magic and the magic of a glittering city on the eve of the Great Crash.

Hapgood, Norman, and Henry Moskowitz. *Up from the City Streets* (Grosset & Dunlap, 1927). The early years of Alfred E. Smith. The great governor is, sadly, rapidly becoming lost to history as the last of his intimates die, but he is one of the most poignant political figures I have ever encountered, and one of the very few who become, the more you know about them, only more wonderful.

Mitgang, Herbert. *The Man Who Rode the Tiger* (J. B. Lippincott, 1963). The man who brought Mayor Jimmy Walker down: Judge Samuel Seabury. This stern, upright moralist is generally unknown today, but is well worth reading about. A fine picture, as well, of an exemplar of a generation almost no one remembers: the great reformers of New York.

Warner, Emily Smith. *The Happy Warrior* (Doubleday, 1956). One might shrink from reading a daughter's adoring biography of her father, but this father is Al Smith, who deserves to be adored, and his daughter gives a vivid picture not only of him but of life in the teeming Irish tenement districts of the Lower East Side in which he grew up.

Bibliography

One of the concerns of my work is the use of economic power to create political power. I have found it rather difficult to learn about this subject because there is little good writing on it. Here are five books that have helped me:

Josephson, Matthew. *The Robber Barons* (Harcourt, Brace, and Company, 1934), and Josephson, M., *The Politicos, 1865–1896* (Harcourt, Brace, 1938). The best, I believe, on the subject.

Lundberg, Ferdinand. *America's Sixty Families* (Citadel, 1937). Still one of the better analyses of the use of economic power to create political power.

Noonan, John T. *Bribes* (Macmillan, 1984). A recent book, little publicized. Unusual in that it is a work whose author has taken a vast subject —the buying and selling of public influence—and attempted to examine its every implication, not only political and economic but moral and philosophical, trying to encompass the whole subject throughout history and to go to its very roots.

Overacker, Louise. *Money in Elections* (Macmillan, 1932). Money in politics, its uses and abuses, from the Medicis to the Republican party of the 1920s. No one else has done work in this field that is as thorough as this book by Professor Overacker.

Because I was a native New Yorker, learning about Texas and its people was not easy. Although many scores of books have been written on the Lone Star State, I found that only a handful were lastingly helpful to me. They include:

Fehrenbach, T. R. *Lone Star: A History of Texas and the Texans* (Macmillan, 1968). A vivid and dramatic narrative that explains better than any other the state and its people as I found them.

Graves, John. *Hard Scrabble* (Alfred A. Knopf, 1974). A memoir of life in the Hill Country of Texas.

Humphrey, William. *Farther Off from Heaven* (Alfred A. Knopf, 1977). A brilliantly written, poignant account of life in a small cotton town in Texas and of a boy who grew up there.

Hunter, John Marvin, and George W. Saunders. *The Trail Drivers of Texas* (The Southwest Press, 1929). This is a huge collection of firsthand memoirs from the last of the old trail drivers. A lot of reminiscences are dull, but buried in them are unusual details and the flavor of what life in post–Civil War Texas was really like.

247]

Key, V. O. *Southern Politics in State and Nation* (Alfred A. Knopf, 1949). A book whose author did an unusually thorough job of portraying a subject of Byzantine complexity.

Olmsted, Frederick Law. *A Journey Through Texas, or, A Saddletrip on the Southwestern Frontier* (Edwards & Co., 1857). The great maker of parks was also a fine maker of words, as I discovered when I picked this book up in the course of trying to learn about life in the Southwest before the Civil War.

Webb, Walter Prescott. *The Great Frontier* (Houghton Mifflin, 1952), and Webb, W. P., *The Great Plains* (Ginn & Co., 1931). Aspects of life on the lonely farms and ranches of the Southwest as you won't find it in the movies.

Until I began my biography of Robert Moses, *The Power Broker,* I had not thought that there was anything inherently fascinating in roads and highways in and of themselves. How wrong I was, as these books taught me:

Bureau of Public Roads. *When All Roads Led to Rome* (Bureau of Public Roads, n.d.). The roads of Rome—a study that might have been dull, had not the subject of their conception and construction been so inherently glorious.

Isaacs, Edith. *Love Affair with a City* (Random House, 1967). A memoir of Stanley Isaacs, the reformer who built the only highway ever constructed in New York that was built with consideration of the residents living near it.

Schreiber, Hermann. *Merchants, Pilgrims, and Highwaymen: A History of Roads Through the Ages* (G. P. Putnam's Sons, 1962).

Finally, I recommend all of Francis Parkman, most notably *Montcalm and Wolfe.* I include his books because I keep copies next to my desk to remind me of two things: first, that it is the job of a historian to try to write at the same level as the greatest novelists, and second, that it is the duty of a historian to go to the locales of the events that will be described and not to leave, no matter how long it takes, until the writer has done his or her best to understand the locales and their cultures and their people.

Contributors

ROBERT A. CARO was born and raised in New York City and
its suburbs, and, after winning several journalistic awards there as an
investigative reporter, spent seven years writing his first book—about the
man who shaped much of the city. *The Power Broker: Robert Moses and
the Fall of New York* (1975) has been acclaimed as a modern American
classic. It won the Pulitzer Prize in Biography and the Francis Parkman
Prize, awarded annually by the Society of American Historians to the
book which "best represents the union of the historian and the artist." For
his next project, a three-volume biography, *The Years of Lyndon Johnson*,
Mr. Caro chose to write about a man who grew up in a very different
world, and for a good part of the seven years that it took to research and
write the first volume of the trilogy—*The Path to Power*—he and his wife,
Ina, moved to the Hill Country of Texas. The book won many awards,
including the National Book Critics Circle Award as the best nonfiction
work of 1982. He is now at work on the second and third volumes. A
graduate of Horace Mann School and Princeton University, Mr. Caro
was a Nieman Fellow at Harvard University and is past president of the
Authors Guild of America.

DAVID McCULLOUGH, who was born in Pittsburgh and
educated there and at Yale, wrote his first book, *The Johnstown Flood*,

while working as an editor at American Heritage. His most recent book, *Mornings on Horseback*, the life of the young Theodore Roosevelt, won the American Book Award for biography. He is also the author of *The Great Bridge*, a widely acclaimed narrative history of the building of the Brooklyn Bridge, and of *The Path Between the Seas*, about the creation of the Panama Canal, which was a national best-seller, a main Selection of the Book-of-the-Month Club, and winner of both the National Book Award for History and the Francis Parkman Prize. Mr. McCullough and his wife, the former Rosalee Barnes, have five children and live in Washington, D.C., where he serves as host of the Emmy Award-winning PBS television series *Smithsonian World*.

P A U L C . N A G E L , before realizing that he was meant to be a biographer, spent twenty years teaching and writing about the history of ideas—an interest that led to *One Nation Indivisible: The Union in American Thought* and *This Sacred Trust: American Nationality 1798–1898*. In a departure that veered close to autobiography, *Missouri*, Mr. Nagel described the spirit of his native state. He then settled down as a biographer of families, starting with *Descent From Glory: Four Generations of the John Adams Family*, meanwhile also serving as director of the Virginia Historical Society. His next book will be *From Abigail to Clover: Stories of the Adams Women*, which will appear in 1987, after which he will devote himself to another distinguished group, the Lees of Virginia. He expects that this choice will keep him closer to home, since he and his wife, Joan Peterson, live in Richmond.

R I C H A R D B . S E W A L L says that Millicent Todd Bingham, in her search for a biographer of Emily Dickinson, "made it abundantly clear, both before and after the mantle fell on me, that criterion number one was a New England background. That, at least, I could provide. But what she fastened on was eleven generations of New England clergymen (all but one Congregational). Schooling in New Hampshire (Exeter), college in Massachusetts (Williams) and postgraduate work in Connecticut (Yale) helped to fulfill the geographical requirement. She liked the thought that I had spent every summer of my life, except the years of World War II, on the coast of Maine. She liked it that I was a professor of English at Yale. My writings before she came to her decision had been

Contributors

modest. When my book on tragedy, *The Vision of Tragedy*, was published in 1959, the way was clear for Emily Dickinson—except, that is, for the daily duties I had at Yale." The resulting book, *The Life of Emily Dickinson*, won the National Book Award for 1974.

RONALD STEEL, who was born in Illinois and educated at Northwestern and Harvard, has written extensively on American politics and foreign policy. He is a regular contributor to the *New York Review of Books* and a contributing editor of the *New Republic*. His *Walter Lippmann and the American Century* (1982) won the American Book Award, the National Book Critics Circle Award and the Bancroft Prize. He is also the author of several other books, including *Pax Americana*, *Imperialists and Other Heroes* and *The End of Alliance: America and the Future of Europe*. He has worked as a journalist in both Europe and the United States and has taught at a number of American universities, including Yale and the University of Texas. He is now professor of international relations at the University of Southern California.

JEAN STROUSE grew up in Los Angeles, went to Verde Valley School in Sedona, Arizona, and graduated from Radcliffe College in 1967. She has worked at the *New York Review of Books* and at Pantheon Books and was a book critic for *Newsweek* from 1979 to 1983. She edited *Women & Analysis: Dialogues on Psychoanalytic Views of Femininity* and is the author of *Alice James, A Biography* (1980), which won the Bancroft Prize in American History and Diplomacy in 1981. She has held fellowships from the John Simon Guggenheim Memorial Foundation, the National Endowment for the Humanities, the National Endowment for the Arts and the Radcliffe Institute. Her articles and reviews have appeared in *The New Yorker*, the *New York Times*, the *New York Review of Books* and the *Washington Post*. She lives in New York and is now at work on a biography of Pierpont Morgan.

WILLIAM ZINSSER began his career with the New York *Herald Tribune*, spending thirteen years there as a writer, editor and critic. He left the paper in 1959 to become a freelance writer and has since contributed regularly to *The New Yorker* and other leading magazines. From 1968 to 1972 he wrote a column for *Life*. During the 1970s he was

Contributors

---

at Yale University, where he taught nonfiction writing and humor writing and was master of Branford College. He is now general editor of the Book-of-the-Month Club. He is the author of eleven books, including the classic *On Writing Well.* His most recent book is *Willie and Dwike: An American Profile,* a portrait of the jazz musicians Willie Ruff and Dwike Mitchell. A fourth-generation Manhattanite, he lives in his home town with his wife, Caroline Zinsser.